Staff Support Groups in the Helping Professions

Staff burnout and work-related stress in mental health professionals cost the National Health Service not only millions of pounds each year, but also impact upon the welfare of those being cared for. *Staff Support Groups in the Helping Professions* takes the lead from recent Department of Health initiatives, promoting the use of staff support groups to foster emotional resilience, deal with potential conflict and support reflective practice.

In this book Hartley, Kennard and their contributors explore the influences that help and hinder the setting up and running of staff support groups, and attempt to counter the often negative reactions that the term 'staff support' can evoke. They demonstrate that such support groups can be a sophisticated and valuable intervention that needs careful preparation and skilful management to succeed, and will in turn not only benefit the individual, but also the department as a whole and those that they care for.

Contributors share their experiences of facilitating support groups in a number of settings including:

- psychiatric wards
- therapeutic communities
- social services
- schools
- children's homes.

Containing a wealth of case material, *Staff Support Groups in the Helping Professions* will provide much-needed guidance for those professionals attending, managing, or in the process of setting up a staff support group.

Phil Hartley is an Adult Psychotherapist at St Andrews Counselling and Psychotherapy Service, North Yorkshire and York Primary Care Trust. He is also a member of the Institute of Group Analysis.

David Kennard is a clinical psychologist and group analyst providing supervision and staff support to individuals and organizations. He was formerly Head of Psychological Services at The Retreat, York, and is a member of the Institute of Group Analysis.

Staff Support Groups in the Helping Professions

Principles, Practice and Pitfalls

Edited by Phil Hartley and
David Kennard

Routledge
Taylor & Francis Group

LONDON AND NEW YORK

First published 2009 by Routledge
27 Church Road, Hove, East Sussex BN3 2FA

Simultaneously published in the USA and Canada
by Routledge
270 Madison Avenue, New York, NY 10016

Routledge is an imprint of the Taylor & Francis Group, an Informa business

Typeset in Times by Garfield Morgan, Swansea, West Glamorgan
Printed and bound in Great Britain by T J International Ltd, Padstow,
Cornwall
Paperback cover design by Andy Ward

This publication has been produced with paper manufactured to strict
environmental standards and with pulp derived from sustainable forests.

British Library Cataloguing in Publication Data
A catalogue record for this book is available from the British Library

Library of Congress Cataloging in Publication Data
Staff support groups in the helping professions : principles, practice and
pitfalls / edited by Phil Hartley and David Kennard.
        p. cm.
    Includes bibliographical references and index.
    ISBN 978-0-415-44773-7 (hardback) – ISBN 978-0-415-44774-4 (pbk.) 1.
Mental health personnel–Job stress. 2. Burn out (Psychology) 3. Self-help
groups. I. Hartley, Phil (Philip Leslie) 1952- II. Kennard, David, 1944-
    RC451.4.P79S73 2009
    616.89–dc22

                                                        2008043556

ISBN: 978-0-415-44773-7 (hbk)
ISBN: 978-0-415-44774-4 (pbk)

Contents

Editors

Phil Hartley has worked as a psychotherapist for 20 years and is currently Adult Psychotherapist at St Andrews Counselling and Psychotherapy Service, North Yorkshire and York Primary Care Trust. Throughout his career he has specialised in initiating and developing services for people with complex mental health issues in community, secure, and specialist services. He has set up and facilitated staff support groups and supervised other facilitators. He also managed a staff support service in a medium secure unit. Phil is a member of the Institute of Group Analysis and has presented numerous papers about his work at national and international conferences. E-mail address: Phil.Hartley@nyypct.nhs.uk

David Kennard is a clinical psychologist and group analyst providing supervision and staff support to individuals and organizations. Before retiring he was Head of Psychological Services at The Retreat in York from 1992–2004. He has worked in democratic and hierarchical therapeutic communities, in acute and long stay psychiatric wards, in high security settings and in psychotherapy and counselling centres. He is co-author of *An Introduction to Therapeutic Communities* and *A Workbook of Group Analytic Interventions* and co-editor of *Living Together* and *Experiences of Mental Health In-patient Care*. He is currently chair of ISPS UK (the UK network of the International Society for the Psychological Treatments of the Schizophrenias and other psychoses) and is a member of the Institute of Group Analysis. E-mail address: david@dkennard.net

Contributors

Nick Humphreys is Principal Adult Psychotherapist, Humberstone Grange Clinic, Leicester. He is Affiliated to the South Trent Training in Dynamic Psychotherapy. E-mail address: Nick.Humphreys@leicspart.nhs.uk

Bill McGowan is Senior Lecturer (Mental Health) in the School of Nursing and Midwifery, Faculty of Health and Social Sciences at the University of Brighton, Sussex. E-mail address: w.mcgowan77@btinternet.com

Michael Maher is a freelance organisational consultant, psychotherapist and trainer, based in Hampshire. He is a member of the Institute of Group Analysis; and is engaged in further training in Systems-Centered Therapy in the US. E-mail address: mike.maher@homecall.co.uk

Chris Powell is Head of the Tuke Centre and Outpatients, The Retreat, York. He is a group analyst and organisational consultant, and a member of the Institute of Group Analysis. E-mail address: cpowell@thetukecentre.org.uk

Gary Winship is Associate Professor in the School of Education, University of Nottingham. E-mail address: Gary.Winship@nottingham.ac.uk

Ewa Wojciechowska is a group analyst and psychotherapist in private practice and a Director of Relationships at Work Ltd. She is a member of the Institute of Group Analysis. E-mail address: eew@btinternet.com

Foreword

It makes intuitive sense that in health care, support is needed for carers; it is generally acknowledged that happy staff make happy patients. However, the very widespread awareness of this issue is, paradoxically, matched by the equally widespread neglect in thinking about what staff support really should be. This book comes from the authors' willingness to tackle that paradox, apparently with the help of best Yorkshire beer. It is therefore a rare and welcome book, adventuring cautiously into this almost taboo subject area. It is an adventure since staff find taking time to consider their own feelings brings their identity closer to the image of suffering patients than is altogether comfortable. Indeed with the pressure among professional carers to care for others, the pressure to care for themselves is ignored, even frowned upon. And such frowning gets a generous degree of support from efficiency experts and accountants in public services, where direct patient contact is believed to be the only criterion of good professional care. Staff supporting each other appears an indulgence and an escape from the difficulties of the *real* work.

It is only recently that the notion of morale has become influential again, and has still not yet fed through properly into service planning. So often, low morale is regarded as something that should not happen and can in any case be dealt with by a one-off recommendation by an inspection body of some kind. The idea that the personnel and the team are an extremely sensitive working apparatus which needs constant attention and maintenance is resisted, and indeed unwelcome by both professionals who believe themselves to be robust and not nearly as vulnerable as their charges, and by managers called to account for spending the public purse. The book is therefore not only rare and welcome, but also brave since it must squarely confront those two shibboleths.

Anyone familiar with the struggle to offer staff support in the form of a group or team meeting, will be familiar with the often insuperable problems: low or declining attendance, the permanent absence/exclusion of key figures of authority, the persistent reflection on the inadequacy of provision for their work, an obsession with the apparent scandalous inadequacy of other professional groups, the often persistent use of the group for personal abreaction of an individual's distress, and the problem of the group as an arena for developing solidarity around inappropriate beliefs. In short, a staff group can so often simply replicate the clients' problems presented to the service, a process that is often called parallel process.

However, it is not only the ambiguity in the hearts of group members that causes trouble; there is some actual uncertainty when reflecting on what a reflective practice in a staff group actually is. There is always a fault-line when we attempt to meld the personal involvement of individuals with the organisational mode of roles and tasks (e.g. Hinshelwood 2008). This leads to a tendency to slide to opposite poles: the individual experiences of the work on one hand, and on the other the organisation's less personal demands in terms of a role (often written out as a depersonalised job description, etc). The individual's feelings at one pole, and the organisation's purpose at the other appear separate and even conflictual. But, in truth, when we come to the performance of a care role, the person and the role are not easily separated. We are very aware of that fact – the personal is professional; and one cannot do the work of professional care without really acknowledging the personal impact of stress. Such enmeshment can be a productive stress; potentially a guide (our feelings are a 'receiving apparatus') for understanding the precise and vital aspects of the emotional climate. This is the concept of the 'use of self' as some would express it. At the same time, the organisation is inserted deeply inside the individuals – the 'organisation in the mind', which Armstrong (2005) would claim should be the prime focus.

These intimacies between self and organisation frequently lead to confusions about where to focus, and they can surface as unhappy and distracting occurrences in support groups. If the blend of the individual's personal baggage with the burden of the organisational task leads to confusion of the two, then the work of support can dither between a support for the staff member to be his own person, or a support to keep facing the working task. Following on from this, perhaps we could see that various approaches to running staff groups will line up behind one of three different strategies: a focus on the individual's baggage which needs dealing with before the organisational work can be properly attended to; a focus on the impact of the organisational task and conditions upon the staff member, for instance 'role analysis', which unfairly exacerbates the stress of the already stressful work; or, thirdly, a focus on how individuals manage the balancing act between the two, between their stress and the task.

Some, as the authors in this book, would suggest that a successful group moves around amongst these aims (and more), and can flourish as a most flexible entity, applying itself where necessary. Others might argue that such versatility, in a situation already ambiguous and confused, needs to be limited by a constant vigilance and group awareness of what aim is being pursued at any given moment. This and many other dimensions of debate mark out where future thought and discussion must move. There is a long debate to be had. The relative advantages and disadvantages of different approaches, tasks, and indeed degrees of flexibility, need more experience and research. This book represents an impressive start on the issues and keeps our noses firmly to the ground, sniffing out the myriad of specific practical issues and questions. It is an extremely thoughtful first appraisal of the issues which have to become part of a developing psychology of care.

I wish this book had been written decades ago, before I started having to learn for myself the pitfalls and advantages of this work. I guess many readers will have the sense that so many of us have had to do this work without turning to an established body of knowledge and experience. We have each had to re-invent the wheel for ourselves. Now – here is the wheel, at last.

Bob Hinshelwood

Preface

This book has had a six year gestation. In December 2002 the editors ran a pair of workshops at an ISPS UK conference entitled *Making the Acute Ward a Therapeutic Environment*. Ours were among a number of parallel sessions, but to our surprise and to some extent our alarm it seemed that all the conference participants wanted to attend. The workshop notice promised that 'managing feelings appropriately in the group or on the ward can be helpful to effective staff performance'. There was a lot of interest in the idea, but talking to one another was quite difficult, there was little consensus, and there were questions about the style of facilitation. On reflection and not surprisingly the workshops were similar to staff support groups. This set us thinking, and initiated a series of meetings between us at one of York's most congenial pubs. There seemed to be sufficient interest in the subject to warrant writing something, and a search of *Amazon* found no evidence that anyone had yet written a book on staff support groups in the field of health care. We decided to try and write one.

We spent a year discussing over pints and by exchange of emails what the scope and structure of the book should be, and also exploring, painfully at times, our ambivalence about writing it. Our own experience was limited mainly to adult mental health settings, secure and non-secure, so we would need to look for contributors from other backgrounds, although we didn't want it to be just a book of edited contributions. We wanted to write a core section ourselves. Our ambivalence was partly about taking on another commitment, but more about our doubts about how much difference staff support groups really made and the feeling of impotence that they can engender, especially in the prevailing culture of competences and targets.

Here is an exchange of e-mails between us in May 2003:

PHIL: I feel some ambivalence too. Partly the amount of work and finding time. The subject matter, I think, forces one, or at least me, to confront the damage done to people and teams by the work. Despite running staff groups, I'm sceptical about the degree of difference they make. Part of coming to terms with the work is my inability to make a great deal of change. At most, I influence people's experience of their work. I would like to know more about your ambivalence about the subject matter.

DAVID: My ambivalence – what's it about? One is the overload of commitments right now, which should ease by end June if I can get on with them. Another is my response to the near collapse of the staff support group on X ward, which has been cancelled more often than it's met in the last two to three months, and has felt superficial and been poorly attended when it has met. The nurse manager has been off sick for over a month. I probably need peer supervision on this. Like you I have doubts about the effectiveness of staff groups – partly because they're like a dipstick into the grinding of the organisation's social unconscious, and it's lonely and hellish down there – no one wants to go. Even writing that helps.

PHIL: Since our meeting with Eva and Graeme I think I understand the ambivalence a little better. I was more reassured about individual comments by people who attended the workshop at the ISPS conference . . . I think the participants' disappointment in the workshop was the failure to provide a magical solution. Staff groups also want magical solutions, as do organisations. I think the facilitator's role is to survive being disappointing in order to help staff tolerate their own disappointment in not being able to provide a 'cure'. The culture is one of being constantly just good enough, if lucky. The book, I think, will achieve its task if it allows discussion of failure and disappointment and how it affects staff and the treatment they provide.

And a little later:

PHIL: Heretical management speak this may be but what is wrong with flying in the face of NSF [National Service Framework] and NICE [National Institute for Health and Clinical Excellence]! What we are trying to write, I think, is how to actually get on and achieve a task. Bureaucratic systems do not contemplate failure because they rely on procedure not process – we should concentrate on process.

It took us the best part of two years to resolve our ambivalence sufficiently to agree a format for the book and begin looking for contributors and a publisher. The rest of the time was taken up with developing the book's structure and content, long exchanges with our contributors, and finally writing and debating our own chapters. Such is the nature of writing collaborations. We hope we and our contributors have managed to steer a middle way between the extremes of despair and magical (or procedural) solutions, and to provide a balance of practical, truthful realism about the experience of working in caring settings and demonstrating that sharing these experiences, if carefully managed, can help to ease the pain and improve the quality of care staff are able to give.

Phil Hartley
David Kennard
York
July 2008

Acknowledgements

I would like to thank a number of people without whom I would have been unlikely to write and edit my parts of the book. The book was David Kennard's idea, and I am particularly grateful that he asked me to co-write and edit it with him. David has been an enormous inspiration and highly capable tutor, who has patiently helped with my writing. I have enjoyed working and thinking with him and commend him to anyone embarking on writing a book. I would like to thank my wife Helen for her constant support and encouragement, my stepson Lewis who did some of the typing with skills that put mine to shame, and my two daughters Anna and Ruth who entertained themselves and put up with me being shut in a room, away from the hubbub of family life. My contribution to the book was quite a family affair. Lastly and by no means least I would like to thank Christine for her patient and skilled typing of draft after draft of my handwriting.

Phil Hartley

I asked Phil Hartley to write this book with me as I did not have enough first hand experience to do it on my own, and I knew and respected the breadth and depth of Phil's work in this area, some of which I had experienced at first hand. The partnership has been a mutually rewarding and enjoyable learning experience. We set out to write four chapters each but in the end they have all been more or less collaborative efforts. Going further back I would like to thank several former colleagues in Oxford who formed my first and most important reference group for developing my interest in staff group dynamics, in particular Lucy Agerholme, Peter Agulnik, Danny Fordwor, Bertram Mandelbrote, Beau Stevenson and Steve Wilson. I would also like to thank Gill Moss at The Retreat who helpfully and efficiently obtained copies of papers I needed.

David Kennard

We would both like to thank the following people for their help and encouragement at various stages in producing this book: Keith Coupland, Graeme Farquharson, Mark Hardcastle, Bill McGowan and Ewa

Wojciechowska. We would like to acknowledge as the inspiration for our title Peter Hawkins' and Robin Shohet's excellent book *Supervision in the Helping Professions*. Lastly we would like to thank all the staff we have worked with in staff support groups over the years, from whom we have learned so much about what helps and what doesn't, and from whom we go on learning.

Introduction

Articles about support groups for nurses, psychiatrists and medical students first started appearing in medical and nursing journals in the 1970s and early 1980s (Kanas 1986), yet to our knowledge this is the first book devoted exclusively to the topic of staff support groups in the helping professions. Why should this be so – that a topic with a 30 year history has not invited the detailed attention that a book can give?

Perhaps one answer lies in the ambivalence the topic arouses concerning the gap between our wish for a powerful agent to reduce pressure and anxiety at work, and the feeling of impotence that nothing we do makes much difference. (Perhaps surprisingly the research evidence we present in Chapter 8 suggests that around half those attending staff support groups do find them helpful.)

Another answer may be that staff support groups are a little like mongrels: there are a lot of them around but they don't have the pedigree of therapeutic groups, supervision groups or sensitivity groups. Although their owners may regard them with much fondness, they are not subject to the same kind of scrutiny, evaluation and public presentations. And like mongrels, staff support groups may have a mixture of antecedents which makes them hard to categorise. They can sometimes be sturdy and long-lived, but people are inclined to give little thought to their care and often abandon them when they lose interest.

The aims of this book are to give a brief overview of the origins and spread of staff support groups, to indicate their value and uses, and to provide a practical guide to their effective management and facilitation, and the pitfalls that await the unprepared. We think that much can be done to avoid or reduce the factors that work against their success and to increase the likelihood of staff finding such groups beneficial.

Although we hope that the book will be of value to anyone embarking on, or already involved in, this important and neglected aspect of group work, we think we should caution the reader that facilitating staff support groups is not something to be undertaken by an inexperienced group worker, and that the book should not be treated as a manual. As we hope will become clear, the task is one that calls for an appreciation of what is going on at different levels in an organisation, openly and covertly, from the individual through to the team and up to the organisation's management structure and leadership. It calls for a combination of understanding, tact and tenacity that at times will stretch even the most experienced group practitioner.

Having issued this caution, we hope the book will be of real and practical use to anyone who does engage in, or seek a better understanding of, this challenging, important and rewarding work.

We do not attempt to create a unified theoretical model for staff support groups – if we accept they are group 'mongrels' that might be a logical contradiction. We do try to locate their place in relation to other kinds of groups in the helping professions, and to provide what we think are sensible and tested approaches to setting up staff support groups and getting the best out of them.

THE PREVALENCE OF STAFF SUPPORT GROUPS

Staff support groups can be found in the following settings:

- acute psychiatric wards;
- units for people with long-term mental health problems;
- community mental health teams;
- secure forensic units, special hospitals and offender institutions;
- therapeutic communities;
- child and adolescent services;
- psychotherapy and counselling services;
- hospices;
- social services;
- plus a variety of medical and educational settings.

It is hard to get precise figures for the number of staff support groups running at any one time. An informal survey by the editors in preparing this book suggested that anything between two and ten staff support groups or reflective practice groups (we address the different use of these two terms in Chapter 1) were being run in each mental health trust in England. Most of these were in community mental health teams or in more specialist services with a known high risk of stress including secure settings, therapeutic communities, personality disorder services, hospices and women's services. In a survey of 189 schools and departments providing mental health teaching in England, 64 per cent of nurse lecturers reported they were involved in facilitating staff support groups, and the proportions for other disciplines were psychology 46 per cent, occupational therapy 26 per cent, medicine 25 per cent, social work 18 per cent (Ferguson *et al.* 2003).

THE POLICY CONTEXT

In recent years the Department of Health has recognized work-related stress and low staff morale as widespread problems in the health service and has produced initiatives to address them (Department of Health (DH) 2000, 2003). A number of factors have been identified as leading to work-related stress, including lack of autonomy, organisational confusion, staff being isolated from their team, misunderstanding of one another's roles and lack of management support (DH 2003). A number of recent reports include actions for looking after the staff. *Mental Health Policy Implementation Guide: Adult Acute Inpatient Care Provision* emphasises the need to develop a 'culture of learning from the day to day experiences of working with users and their families' (DH 2002: 21). Guidance by the National Institute for Mental Health in England (NIMHE) in 2003, *Personality Disorder: No Longer a Diagnosis of Exclusion*, stresses the need for staff working with this client group to have a high degree of emotional resilience, and for all personality disorder teams to have 'robust structures for supervision that support reflective practice and assist staff to manage anxiety and deal with conflict' (NIMHE 2003: 44).

Excellent models for supervision in mental health work have been developed by Proctor (2000) and Hawkins and Shohet (2000) and the concept of reflective practice (Schon 1991) has emerged as an important feature of training and continuing professional development in the mental health professions – in particular nursing (Ryan and Pritchard 2004; Bulman *et al.* 2004). We believe that staff support groups contribute to the effective functioning of staff teams and the well-being of their members in a way that differs from clinical supervision or from a model of reflective practice based on analysing decision-making processes. The explicit core intention of staff support groups is to help the members of a staff team talk together about the emotional impact of their work and support each other in coping with stressful situations. Although the aim sounds simple, putting it into practice is often quite complex.

WHAT IS THE PROBLEM WITH STAFF SUPPORT GROUPS?

The following statements, not direct quotes but not untypical of what one often hears, give some hint at what the problem might be:

'I feel guilty sitting in a staff support group when there are patients out there that need care.'

'Staff support groups are a management device to get the staff to accept the unacceptable.'

'How can I say what I really feel in front of colleagues I have to work with each day or a manager who'll be doing my appraisal?'

We can see at once that there are complex issues and that ambivalence about taking part in a staff support group might be expected as the norm and the starting point for anyone planning to set up or run such a group.

The jumping off point for this book is therefore a question. Given the strong case for staff support in mental health and related services, and the enthusiasm that many managers and clinical leaders have for staff support groups, why do they often fail? Why do the staff who request them often struggle to use them and let them starve through lack of attendance and attention? We believe that an understanding is needed of the inherent difficulties in setting up and running staff support groups, and for staff in using them, if they are to work effectively. The aim of this book is to balance an optimistic and positive view of the potential benefits of a staff support group with a realistic appreciation of the issues involved that might hinder or torpedo their efforts, and how to think about and deal with these issues.

THEORETICAL UNDERPINNINGS OF THE BOOK

The editors and several of the contributors are group analysts, whose approach combines concepts from psychoanalysis and social psychology – in particular group dynamics and systems theory (Foulkes 1964, 1975; Pines 1983). In addition several of us have worked in therapeutic communities and have derived practical experience of the interface between individuals and institutions from these settings. These connections are no accident – professionals with these backgrounds tend to be the ones who are interested in staff support groups. However, in writing and editing the book we have tried to avoid making theoretical assumptions about the situations we describe – with what success the reader must judge – and to explain the use of psychodynamic concepts where these occur. We are aware that readers may have diverse theoretical backgrounds – psychoanalytic, person-centred, cognitive-behavioural – and hope the book is accessible to all these readers.

THE PLAN OF THE BOOK

The book is divided into two parts. The first part is written by the editors and is intended to provide an overview and practical guide to setting up and facilitating staff support groups. The second part comprises contributions by six experienced facilitators writing about their experiences of facilitating staff support groups in a variety of settings.

Part I

Chapter 1, 'What staff support groups are for', identifies the range of uses staff support groups have and looks at how they differ from other kinds of groups that are designed to help the staff in care-giving settings, such as reflective practice groups, supervision groups and sensitivity groups. We suggest here that it is the flexibility of staff support groups that is both their strength and a potential risk. Chapter 2 tackles a preliminary question that we feel is necessary to address in any book on staff support, whether individual or group: why it is difficult for staff to ask for support, especially if they work in one of the caring professions. Anyone who has tried to set up a system for supporting staff will almost certainly have encountered this paradox – that support needs are readily acknowledged but offers of support are often poorly used. As already suggested above, the reasons for this are complex. In this chapter we try to tease out the factors in the individual, in the team, in the institution, and in the concept of support itself, that influence someone's readiness to use the available support.

Chapter 3 provides the reader with an overview of what we consider are the ten keys to a successful staff support group. We didn't write the chapter with the rounded figure of ten in mind, but that is the number that emerged. This chapter is both a summary and a starting point for the three chapters that follow. It underscores why staff support groups need careful preparation and sensitive facilitation by an experienced group worker if they are to work effectively. Chapter 4 goes into the questions that need to be considered in setting up a staff support group. We do this from two perspectives: the individual or team looking for someone to facilitate a staff support group, and the would-be facilitator. Care and thought at this stage will help to build a group on firm foundations rather than one that collapses early on. Chapter 5 explores the role of the facilitator once the group is up and running, starting with the early sessions, and addressing issues of boundaries, task maintenance and working with feelings. We also touch here on the overlap and differences between facilitating a staff support group and a therapeutic group. Chapter 6 picks up the questions and concerns, identified at the end of Chapter 4, that group members often ask about and explores them in more depth, with examples from practice looking at how they can be responded to. These concerns include the impact of poor or erratic attendance and punctuality on the group, how to deal with silences or distress in the group, or not knowing what to talk about, and the impact of senior staff and managers attending the group.

Chapter 7 deals with the ending of a staff support group. Most groups come to an end at some point, whether imposed by an external change, or because they were set up for a fixed period of time, or are felt to be not working any more. In this chapter we describe different ending scenarios, planned and unplanned. Endings are never easy, but we try to show that, as with any relationship, how the ending is managed can make a big difference to what individuals take away from the experience.

The final chapter in Part I addresses the question, 'Do staff support groups work?' Although outcome research in this field is thin on the ground, our search of the literature of the past two decades found around a dozen studies that had attempted a systematic evaluation of some kind. The conclusions we were able to draw are that well set up and well run staff support groups are experienced as beneficial, and that even where these conditions are not fully met, staff groups with an external facilitator are likely to be experienced as helpful by around half of those taking part. We examine the factors that influence whether groups are experienced as helpful. The chapter begins with a summary of each of the studies found and then pulls together the findings and their implications in the discussion section.

Part II

In Part II we invited a number of experienced staff group facilitators from different professional backgrounds to write about their experiences in different settings. Each chapter begins with an introduction by the editors which links it with topics and issues discussed in Part I. In Chapter 9 Bill McGowan gives an engrossing session-by-session account of a staff support group he was invited to run on a busy acute admission ward in a psychiatric setting. Although the group ended after its initial six-month trial period, the difficulties and the achievements in running the group in the face of the enormous pressures the staff faced, and the lessons learned, are vividly portrayed in McGowan's account.

Work with the staff of local authority children's homes is the setting for Chapter 10 by Michael Maher. Maher offered staff support groups to eight homes, an offer that was eagerly seized by some managers but responded to with wariness by others. He describes the stressful nature of the staff's work and provides useful theory–practice links to Foulkes' group-analysis and to Agazarian's systems-centered model of group work, using the latter to discuss the pervasive impact of authority issues and subgroups. Maher also examines the nature of his own relationship with the organisation's management structure.

In Chapter 11 Chris Powell focuses on an issue touched on in Part I and in Maher's chapter: facilitating a staff support group in an organisation in which the facilitator also has a clinical or managerial role. Readers who find themselves in (or potentially in) this situation will find this chapter of great value as Powell examines his experiences and dilemmas both in the group and in his relationships with other managers in the wider organisation, and reflects on the pros and cons of working in this way.

In Chapter 12 Ewa Wojciechowska draws on her experience in different care settings in the statutory and voluntary sectors, to examine an issue that affects all staff who work in care-giving roles: the boundary between one's professional role and personal feelings and experience. How we each deal with this juxtaposition of the personal and the professional, our understanding of why we do the kind of work we do and how our work affects us, are crucial to our effectiveness as professionals and to our own personal well-being. Wojciechowska's vignettes vividly portray these issues, and also explore those situations where the facilitator may decide to meet with a member of staff outside the group.

As in Powell's chapter, in Chapter 13 Nick Humphreys writes from the perspective of an insider, in this case a senior member of staff in a therapeutic community. He describes the way the staff group can become 'infected' with feelings or states of mind that come from the work with clients with histories of traumatic relationships, and demonstrates interventions that can initiate in the staff group the thoughtful discussion that is needed for the team to explore its responses and return to a healthier level of functioning.

In the final chapter Gary Winship recounts his experience of being invited to offer support to teachers in a day-cum-boarding school for 11- to 18-year-olds following a spate of self-harm among the pupils. Winship describes in vivid detail his initial exploratory meeting with the staff, and examines why the dynamics that emerged may have led to the rejection of further help, and whether the outcome could have been different.

The book ends with a brief conclusion by the editors, in which we propose that the core knowledge and skills needed for facilitating staff support groups should be treated as seriously as those required for supervision and management.

PART I

Chapter 1

What staff support groups are for

David Kennard and Phil Hartley

Staff support groups are for staff who work closely together under conditions of some stress – e.g. on a hospital ward, in a children's unit, a secure unit or a hospice. They may be set up in response to a perceived problem in the staff team, or as part of a general policy for staff support and development. They are generally created with the twin aims of helping team members as individuals to cope with the stresses of the job, and helping the team as a whole to work better together.

In attempting to define the aims of staff support groups we meet the mix of straightforwardness and fuzziness that the reader will come to recognize as a feature. The following statements (some taken from other writers, some our own) address different aspects of what staff support groups are for.

1   *To promote the value and the practice of open communication.* Although we can all agree in principle with the importance of good communication between team members, there are often obstacles to translating this into practice. Some obstacles are practical (not enough time, too much information), others can arise between individuals – e.g. disagreements, feeling slighted – or in the team as a whole – e.g. low morale, feeing undervalued. Clearing away these obstacles to open communication takes time, commitment and practice.

2   *To provide a protected time and space in which staff can get support from colleagues and learn from each other.* In a busy, pressured environment, the commitment to spend one hour a week (or some comparable time) away from the coal face in a quiet, preferably undisturbed room, without a clinical or business agenda to get through, provides the opportunity to 'touch base' – with colleagues and with oneself – and to develop the skills of open communication. Arguably it is the fact of the existence of this fixed, protected time 'for the staff' that is as important as what goes on within it.

3   *'To improve staff well-being in ways that are associated with better patient care and smoother unit functioning'* (Lederberg 1998: 276). Lederberg cautions that the demands of high-stress medical units

require some suppression of feelings by the staff, and that it is the job of the support group in such settings to help maintain the viability of the work setting, and not to probe feelings except where these are harming the individual or the task.

4   *To enable staff to express, discuss and manage difficult or painful emotional responses – such as guilt or anxiety – to people and situations in their work.* 'Difficult interactions with patients leave us with subjective experiences that are often unpleasant. We feel things, for example, frustrated, inadequate or angry. If we act on these feelings directly we run the risk of acting unprofessionally' (Haigh 2000: 312). Haigh is explaining the need for staff sensitivity groups. Although staff support groups are different in some ways (see below) the point is equally relevant. We owe it to ourselves, our colleagues and our patients/clients to be aware of our personal reactions to our experiences at work, and to cope with them in ways that don't end up compromising the help we offer, our working relationships, or our own health and well-being.

5   *'To enable staff to use the full range of their emotional responses in the service of the task – not to have to protect themselves by shutting down emotionally'* (Farquharson 2003). This expands the above aim. One way of coping is to switch off *all* our feelings, just to get through the day. The problem with this is that it means we also switch off our sensitivity to others' feelings and emotional states. We can miss cues, and be experienced as brusque or giving inappropriate responses. In providing the opportunity to become aware of their emotional responses, staff support groups can help staff to cope with their own reactions in more constructive ways.

6   *'To create an environment where the vulnerable parts of ourselves, which have been shielded by our defences, can be responded to and understood'* (Rifkind 1995: 211). Rifkind points out that we may be afraid of revealing our feelings because it would leave us vulnerable to criticism, or give the impression of not coping. She notes that in a staff group 'we feel the pressure to claim that we are coping with change and doing a good job'. Enabling staff to acknowledge their vulnerable sides without this being seen as a sign of weakness or needing special help – normalising vulnerability – is a core aim of a staff support group.

7   *To enable the team to discuss obstacles to team working that may arise from issues between individuals, within the team as a whole, or between the team and the wider organisation.* This last aim is a catch-all that may more properly belong with a group set up specifically to explore staff team relations, group dynamics or organisational issues. However, where these are clearly impinging on a team's functioning or on staff well-being, the staff support group can address the problem.

The reader will see that the above aims range from ones that would be widely accepted as a 'good thing' through to those that deal with more deep seated, harder to reach aspects of a team's experience. Bolton and Roberts (1994: 157) have found it useful to distinguish between three levels in the aims of staff support groups. There are the *overt*, publicly stated aims (e.g. to improve staff communication), there may be *covert* aims which are known to some participants but are not openly acknowledged (e.g. to cope with a difficult team member, to push through unpopular changes), and there may also be *unconscious* aims which 'remain to be discovered'. We will return to these levels in looking at different agendas in responding to requests for a staff support group in Chapter 4.

HOW STAFF SUPPORT GROUPS DIFFER FROM OTHER KINDS OF STAFF GROUPS

Another element of fuzziness we have to negotiate is the lack of clear distinctions between different kinds of staff groups. Many labels are used for groups that are created to help staff in care-giving settings with their work. You may have come across the following:

- case discussion group;
- continuing professional development group;
- consultation group;
- experiential group;
- personal development group;
- process group;
- reflective practice group;
- seminar group;
- sensitivity group;
- staff support group;
- supervision group;
- training group.

It doesn't help that these terms are only a loose guide to what actually happens in a group. It is likely that some groups that are similar in practice will have different names, while groups with the same name may operate differently from each other.

A name may be chosen for a variety of reasons. One of the authors was invited to run a 'supervision group' on a hospital ward but soon realised that what was wanted was more like a staff support group, exploring communication issues within the team. It seemed that calling it supervision may have helped the group feel more 'contained' and task-focused. (Avoiding the term 'support' is taken up in Chapter 2.)

In what follows we give what we see as the main attributes of the more commonly used terms, and in doing so try to highlight what is distinctive about staff support groups.

Reflective practice groups

The concept of the reflective practitioner was introduced in the 1980s by Donald Schon (Schon 1984). Reflective practice has become widely used in higher education and in the training of health professionals including nurses, midwives, physiotherapists and clinical psychologists. Reflective practice has been described as a process by which the practitioner should stop and think about their practice, consciously analyse their decision-making processes, and relate theory to what they do in practice. This can take place in different ways, e.g. keeping a diary, peer review, in clinical supervision and through significant incident analysis. It can also take place in groups, either in the context of a training course, or in the everyday practice of a team or a hospital ward.

Our impression is that in some settings the term 'reflective practice group' nowadays refers to what would have been called a 'staff support group' 10 or 20 years ago. The change in name in this case may reflect more a change in fashion than in actual practice. Both staff support and reflective practice groups provide an agreed time and place to step outside the work with clients to reflect on what was done and the feelings aroused. Both encourage sharing of experiences, drawing on and learning from colleagues' experience. Where differences occur, they are most likely to be in the degree of structure and the role of the facilitator. The reflective practice group may be more structured, with a timed format ending with an action plan. The structure will also encourage members to maintain a degree of emotional detachment. The facilitator may take a tutorial role, bringing in relevant policies, theories and evidence. By contrast a staff support group is relatively unstructured, encouraging the expression of emotional responses, and the facilitator is likely to focus on members learning from their own and each other's experience.

Sensitivity groups

As with reflective practice, the term 'sensitivity group' is sometimes used interchangeably with staff support group. Again the aims are similar – to help staff be aware of and cope with their personal responses to challenging people and situations. However, a sensitivity group explicitly focuses on the personal relationships and dynamics within the team, and requires a commitment by the group members to exploring these despite the discomfort this may cause. To the extent that it pursues this exploration a sensitivity group may not be experienced as supportive. However, it has been observed that, 'The measure of efficiency of a staff sensitivity group is not necessarily the amount of support that happens inside the group but the amount of support that happens elsewhere outside of the group' (Winship and Hardy 1999: 309).

Bramley (1990: 302) has offered the following comprehensive definition of the task of a sensitivity group: 'to come to a better understanding of the manifest and latent relationships between, and reciprocal influence of, self, colleagues, clients, the job itself, and any relevant wider context, so as to improve job performance.' Sensitivity groups may be particularly valuable for staff teams that use a psychodynamic approach in their work and who value the exploration of hidden or unconscious elements in personal relationships as a relevant and necessary part of their job.

An important difference between sensitivity and support groups is that in sensitivity groups exploration of staff relationships is a required task, whereas in staff support groups relationships may be explored in the context of a particular issue – e.g. coping with organisational change – or if they are having an effect on team working or well-being, but this is not the primary aim of the group.

Supervision groups

The main aim of supervision is to help practitioners monitor and improve the quality of their work with patients. However, it does also have an important supportive function. In *Supervision in the Helping Professions* Hawkins and Shohet (2000: 22) describe supervision as, 'a central form of support, where we can focus on our own difficulties . . .'. In writing about supervision in groups, Hawkins and Shohet identify three types of supervision group: those that only meet for supervision, those that work as a team but with different clients, and those that work as a team with the same clients. Staff support groups are for the second and third of these and mostly the third – teams who work with the same client group.

Supervision groups are also likely to function differently from staff support groups. Groups may be quite small (typically 3–5 supervisees) with the focus clearly on individual learning. There may be explicit agreements on the supervisees' and supervisor's roles and responsibilities in the group, and different formats according to the members' level of development (Proctor 2000). Members usually take it in turns to present a case, which is then discussed by the group with the supervisor facilitating the discussion and helping the group to make theory–practice links according to the therapeutic model being practised. Case discussion groups are similar to supervision groups but may focus more on the particular issues raised by the case presented rather than on wider learning of therapeutic concepts and practice.

Structured learning groups

Staff seminars and training groups are likely to follow a predetermined format and to deal with a topic of general relevance to the work of the team but not with particular people or situations. They can be used in settings where there is not enough staff continuity for one of the above groups, or where a safer way of bringing a staff team together is needed than one that may be experienced as too intrusive or exposing for staff to accept (see Chapter 2).

Experiential groups

At the other end of the spectrum these groups quite explicitly focus on experiences and issues in the members' personal as well as professional lives, both in the present and the past. Such groups tend to work best as 'stranger' groups where members do not have to be concerned about the impact of self-disclosures on their working relationships with colleagues. Experiential groups are often used as part of training courses in those forms of psychological therapy where personal self-awareness is recognized as a vital component of the learning.

THE FLEXIBILITY OF STAFF SUPPORT GROUPS

The types of group described above are aimed at improving practice by focusing on a particular aspect of a staff team's work: reflective practice focuses on broad educational aims and decision-making processes; sensitivity groups focus on team relationships and dynamics; supervision groups focus on the experience and practice of a particular therapeutic approach.

The focus of the staff support group is less specific. It is more like the lubricant that keeps all the different parts of the engine working efficiently and without friction. To do this it can visit any aspect of the staff team's working life that is causing stress or friction: a painful or difficult experience with a particular client, an awkward or conflictual relationship between two colleagues, an unhelpful split within the team as a whole, an organisational or policy issue that is impacting on the work. In going to one or other of these topics the group draws on the members' experience and ideas, encourages open discussion of the problem and of how to approach or manage it.

This flexibility is both a strength and a risk for the staff support group. A strength because the group can tackle whatever is affecting the well-being of the staff, individually or as a team. At different times it may work rather like a reflective practice group, a sensitivity group or a supervision group, moving in and out of these tasks according to the needs of the group. But it is also a risk because this very flexibility can make it hard to judge if the group is on target or is getting distracted into an unproductive or irrelevant discussion. There may be anxiety in the group over the unpredictability of its focus and whether it will lead to members feeling uncomfortably exposed. To overcome, or at least reduce these risks requires clear ground rules and understandings about the aims and limits of the group and quite skilful facilitation – to be addressed in the following chapters.

The flexibility of staff support groups also means that they can sometimes be set up mistakenly or inappropriately. Bolton and Roberts point out that 'such groups are often requested as an off-the-peg solution to an ill-defined problem for which they are not appropriate' (Bolton and Roberts 1994: 156). It is not only staff support groups that can suffer this fate. In her witty and perceptive account Bramley (1990) describes her experiences of groups that were set up ostensibly as sensitivity groups but where something else was really needed, such as a supervision group or a staff business meeting. The preliminary discussions and negotiation in setting up a staff support group are therefore particularly important, and will be addressed in detail in Chapter 4.

SUMMARY

This chapter sets out the range of aims a staff support group can have and the main differences with other types of group that focus on a particular aspect of a team's work, such as reflective practice groups, sensitivity groups and supervision groups. Whereas each of these have their explicit tasks, staff support groups have the flexibility to focus on whatever problems or relationships issues are affecting the team's effectiveness or well-being at a particular time or in relation to a particular challenge. This flexibility is a strength but also brings certain risks and challenges that need to be recognized and carefully managed if the group is going to achieve its goal of supporting the staff.

Having set out a rough guide to the territory covered by staff support groups the logical next step is to consider how to set one up. Before we do that, however, we should pause to consider the resistance often encountered when providing support for members of the helping professions. Or to put it the other way round, the reluctance that we ourselves can experience in asking for or accepting support at work – individually or in groups.

Chapter 2

Why it can be difficult to ask for support, especially if you work in a caring profession

Phil Hartley and David Kennard

Many people find it difficult to ask for support. In this respect the caring professions, which employ a huge range of people with a wide variety of experiences, are not dissimilar to the general population. Attitude, experience and the setting they are in all make it more or less challenging to do so. This chapter will discuss the reasons why it can be hard for an individual who works in the caring professions to request support and how the workplace affects that.

In our experience of running staff support groups, the people who use them struggle to ask for support from one another. Members of the caring professions understandably see their primary task as looking after others, and not one another, yet many are adversely affected by their work.

Difficulties in asking for support may be a product of:

- a person's individual experience;
- relationships within the teams and organisation;
- the response to identification with clients by the individual and their organisation;
- seeing work-related stress as normal;
- avoiding the term 'support group';
- institutional defences against anxiety.

A PERSON'S INDIVIDUAL EXPERIENCE

A number of writers (Bamber 2006; Bion 1961; Khaleelee 1994; Obholzer and Roberts 2006) have suggested that people can enter the helping professions to manage unresolved issues from childhood. This is not to say that childhood experiences always have a negative effect on adult functioning. They may be useful and even an asset in the helping professions. For example, the experience of having needy and emotionally demanding parents requiring their children to act in a parental capacity may be something that a member of the caring professions can use to become expert at coping with emotionally demanding situations and people. It can become problematic, however, when staff with this expertise rely on it as their major form of validation. They may be particularly vulnerable during specific personal difficulties, for example, divorce, separation, or bereavement, and can be more vulnerable to feeling incompetent or disapproved of during particularly stressful episodes at work. They may in general be at greater risk of work-related stress and emotional or psychological injury.

A person's capacity to deal with such issues is influenced by a number of factors, including previous experience, the severity of the stressful event and the distance from other stresses. The supportive or unsupportive behaviour by a very close other is a major influence in how someone manages psychological crisis (Harris 1992). The caring professional who parented their own needy parent may, for example, have had good enough nurturing experiences of their own from a validating grandparent or other relative who they could turn to. The professional's ability to ask for support is thus influenced by their own experience of being supported by a very close other.

Another scenario may be when a child whose primary role in the family is to moderate conflict between parents becomes a skilled moderator in managing conflict in teams. The team may feel they can rely on them to function in this role, placing them in an impossible and impractical position. In some circumstances, the moderator's failure to do so may lead to an overwhelming sense of disaster originating from childhood fears of parental separation.

During any particularly difficult episode, which may be accompanied by stress in someone's personal life, to ask for support and to receive it is to allow oneself to be temporarily dependent. Unmet needs for protracted periods can lead to a number of potentially serious problem behaviours. Although these are most often recognized in the clients professionals work with, absenteeism, stress-related illness, alcohol and drug problems, and even on rare occasions suicide, are not unfamiliar in professionals who work in the caring professions.

RELATIONSHIPS WITHIN THE TEAM AND ORGANISATION

Punter (2007: 100) discussing staff support groups notes that, 'there can be rivalry and fear of judgement by peers or managers, and investment in fighting, that gets in the way as a group'. Nitsun (1996) discussing mental health professionals' experience of work settings, stresses that teams can cause considerable emotional turmoil. Many people do not experience the team they work in as supportive, but rather rivalrous and on occasions destructive. It is not surprising that people do not want to admit to vulnerability in this climate. Individuals are particularly anxious at how managers might respond to perceived weakness. Most people would prefer to discuss their need for support with an individual, rather than with a group of colleagues. However, Punter (2007: 100) goes on to say that, 'there is a failure to see that the staff group can help each other deal with feelings, by sharing and working together', and Nitsun (1996: 92) says that 'work groups tend to arouse considerable feelings of affiliation as well as rivalry and competition'. Paradoxically, it is the team members who have much of the experience and coping strategies to help one another, but whose anxiety about staff support groups, and the often negative experience of teams, makes it difficult to access.

Professionals in caring settings take with them their own formative experiences of being supported and of dependency, including their historical and habitual means of coping. Most readers will recognize someone in the workplace who operates at one or other end of a dependency continuum: the person who is frequently distressed and needy, or the one who never seems overwhelmed or vulnerable and is always in control. Most people are somewhere in the middle, or move up and down the scale depending on events in their personal and professional lives. The manner in which their dependency needs are expressed is likely to vary according to the individual's personal experience and how the workplace responds.

The response of the workplace is most commonly found in the reaction of a manager to an individual or colleague. The ability of the manager to empathise can influence whether people can allow themselves to be dependent. This does not always mean their dependency needs can be met by the organisation. For example, a manager may not be available to give the type and frequency of support that someone needs, because of organisational constraints placed on him or her. Prolonged experience of this will make it more difficult for individuals to risk depending on their manager. Rivalrous and destructive teams and their managers are perhaps the worst places for individuals to admit to perceived weakness, and ask for support. The fear of a negative invalidating response is too great and probably realistic.

A common fear for health professionals is that they will be seen as too weak to look after their vulnerable clients at times of stress. This is not dissimilar to the parent or carer who is often faced with no choice but to carry on with their task. There is not the time to think of oneself, without risking feeling overwhelmed, and then fearing being unable to continue. Many caring professionals will recognize this as a 'normal' part of their daily routine.

THE RESPONSE TO IDENTIFICATION WITH CLIENTS BY THE INDIVIDUAL AND THEIR ORGANISATION

In some caring professions, particularly in mental health services, the line between the carer and the client can become blurred. This blurring is exacerbated when the professional is experiencing the same or similar feelings as their clients. Lederberg (1998: 286) in discussing this dynamic describes it as, 'worsened by the pull of psychological regression or the fleeting panic that this could be me'. We have heard many nurses, social workers and doctors worrying that if they break down they will be the same as their clients. Although most readers might not think this to be true, most will know of a colleague who appears to mirror their client's problems. Teams are aware of this, but struggle to discuss it or to know what to do about it. Caring professionals resonate with aspects of their client's distress, but worry about admitting it to themselves and their colleagues. It is not surprising that people shy away from discussing their identifications, but by doing so they lose the benefit that Punter (2007) argues is derived from support groups.

In our experience of running staff support groups, people attending and realising that they often feel similarly to their colleagues, and indeed to other professionals and managers, is one of the main benefits they report. Professionals, like clients, can be left feeling isolated and that they are the only one experiencing difficulty. This feeling increases the sense of failure and impotence, with negative comparisons between themselves and their colleagues – a lack of mutuality (discussed later) which makes asking for help even more problematic. Lederberg (1998: 287) points out that workers who feel isolated at work often have their difficulties compounded by isolation in their personal life.

SEEING WORK-RELATED STRESS AS NORMAL

Hirschhorn (1993: 26) developed the idea of 'normal psychological injuries at work', or the 'normal, expectable hurts that people experience as they try to collaborate with others in implementing an organisation's primary task within an uncertain environment'. It is not unusual within organisations to experience psychological injury, for example, anxiety, rejection or feeling threatened. Normal injury is exacerbated in times of change, at least because of increased anxiety and at worst, because of the threat of redundancy or professional uncertainty.

Seeing psychological injury, whether at work or in one's personal life, as 'normal' may have paradoxical effects. It can make it easier to talk about because there is nothing to be ashamed of, or difficult to talk about because it is so common. Like a common cold, the symptoms are acknowledged, but it is not expected that someone really talks about how bad they feel. Everyone gets a cold, so it is assumed everyone knows how it feels without saying much about it and continues to cope adequately. Organisational change and its consequences are like a cyclic epidemic within the caring professions. Some people have developed immunity, but each new wave of 'change virus' claims a new set of victims. It may be those who struggle with constant anxiety due to change, who have weakened 'immune systems' and have the consequent symptoms. To discuss the illness and its effects can be seen to be making too much of something ordinary, not coping, or as being part of the therapy culture. It is perhaps most difficult for those who implement change to consider their own and other people's responses to the consequent psychological injury.

Some respondents in a study of staff support groups (Thomas 2003) cited as the value of the staff group that it 'it helps me resolve the difficult dynamics in the staff team', and 'meets my needs to address issues that affect me'. It seems that despite the normality of psychological injuries people experience at work, they still can benefit from support from one another, even if they cannot be explicit about it. Bolton and Roberts (1994: 156) encapsulate this saying, 'Support Groups bespeak the hope of getting more from colleagues'.

AVOIDING THE TERM 'SUPPORT GROUP'

When the term 'support' is associated with weakness, or not being up to the job, there may be a temptation to rename the staff support group. Thomas discusses his decision to change the name of a staff support group to 'professional development group', arguing that support is equated with passivity and that the new title helped staff to reflect on their 'roles and responsibilities for their professional development' (Thomas 2003: 32). The *Oxford English Dictionary* (1992) defines passivity as 'suffering action, acted upon, offering no opposition'. Many members of the caring professions subject to organisational and policy changes will identify with feeling and being acted upon. However, the implication of the change of name to professional development is that the emphasis is on coping and developing rather than on reflecting on the impact. Avoidance of the term 'support group' may also reflect a feeling that the idea of supporting others is too much of a burden when staff feel themselves too beleaguered in their work to provide support to each other.

We would prefer to argue that the title staff support group 'does what it says on the tin'. The explicit aim is to support staff in their work. This acknowledges that staff may be psychologically injured by their work and could benefit from support. It is a message within the organisation, and helps to establish a culture of mutuality and empathy. If professionals at different levels in the hierarchy attend the group, the term staff support group denotes that all staff can benefit from support.

INSTITUTIONAL DEFENCES AGAINST ANXIETY THAT MAKE IT HARDER TO ASK FOR SUPPORT

Menzies' frequently cited work (Menzies 1959) conceptualised institutional defences against anxiety. She argued that when performing physical and often intimate tasks staff focused on the procedure rather than the experience and the interaction between them and the patient. The weighted emphasis toward the procedure, rather than the experience, becomes less anxiety provoking as emotional distance is put between the operator and the recipient. The caring professions are full of procedures and bureaucracy, for example, appraisals, risk management, contingency planning, improving performance at work policies and aspirational interviews during organisational restructuring. Performance is often measured against how effectively organisational policies and procedures are enacted. Thus, the attention is on the efficacy of the procedure, and not the impact of it. In this climate empathy is much more difficult to develop and sustain, because the emphasis is on the task and not the person. It is like reading about choreography and expecting to be able to choreograph a ballet without understanding the dancer and their relationships to the music and one another. One has to know how to work with performers to get the best from them and interpret the music with emotion and not mechanically. During a climate of constant change that is implemented in terms of new procedures, organisations and their employees can find it increasingly difficult to ask for support because the emotional consequences of change have to be more and more defended against.

Ashton (2007: 94), writing about staff working in haemodialysis, describes institutional defences as 'analogous to individual defences against anxiety, in that they have served people well in the past, or in the institutions' case, in the short term, but in the longer term they are no longer effective, but rather themselves in fact a further cause of anxiety'. Hinshelwood and Skogstad (2005: 166) go further in their unique book using participant-observation methods to study varied but mainly health care settings. They conclude that 'The high level of defensiveness that was found in many of the observed institutions appears to be linked with the apparent lack of containment of anxieties within the organisation'.

Organisations often emphasise staff support as part of their policies and procedures. It is common to see leaflets advertising staff counselling services. Counselling is recommended in policies. Managers can, and do, refer staff for counselling, rather than considering the impact of their work with them. In this scenario the solution becomes part of the problem. Support is used as a human resources response to change, or even as part of a disciplinary process, making asking for and giving support even more difficult. The fact the support is embedded in policy and procedure results in a climate where empathy and mutual support become more and more distant from human interactions (Marrone 1998). The loss of normality and fear of being judged as 'ill' do not create a culture that allows support to be requested. This lack of mutual support can have serious consequences for someone's experience of work. Looking at research in this area Lederberg (1998: 290) concludes that, 'The quality of an individual's social support system at work was found to be one of the strongest predictors of job satisfaction'. The staff support group can be a place to develop mutual support or a social support system. As Lederberg (1998: 295) suggests, 'The group can be an effective holding environment in which care givers support and validate each other around the grief, fear and sense of inadequacy that overwhelm them unpredictably'.

People generally do not want to consider their limitations or their inability to help, but in a caring profession in which the primary task is to offer skilled and effective care, admitting limitations may be even more difficult. Organisations increasingly measured and financed by their successful outcomes do not easily empathise with their employees' real experience of undertaking the organisation's task. In the 'can do' target-driven culture, it becomes more difficult to discuss problems with performing the task, and to acknowledge potential rivalry and envy of those who seemingly do well. The organisation can, in its capacity to deal with its own limitations, make it more or less difficult for its members to empathise with one another and to ask for support. Bamber (2006) argues that organisations can make this possible when psychological support is seen as part of the normal culture of the organisation and senior members of the organisation lead by example, rather that it being something that is stigmatised. Support systems are then more easily developed to help employees cope with their work.

THE PRO-SUPPORT ORGANISATION

It is difficult to ask for support, especially in the caring professions because of a constellation of personal and organisational influences. One's personal history of being empathised with, and having dependency needs met by a 'close other' limits or enhances the caring professional's ability to ask for support. The organisation in which they work can, if it empathises with its members' experience, create a climate whereby it is safe to ask for support. This is most likely when this is a mutual and interpersonal expectation, rather than bureaucratic procedure. Managers of organisations using institutional defences to distance themselves from the reality of their workers' experience, and their own limitations, find it increasingly difficult to ask for and give support other than through policy and procedure.

Some members of the caring professions may be attempting to use the workplace to resolve their formative experiences and others may experience psychological injury. The organisation that recognizes these occurrences as normal is being empathic. Organisational structures that proactively develop staff support groups or systems as a normal part of the working routine are likely to make it easier for employees to request and offer support. Professional training and practice could be enhanced by learning that occasionally not to cope is normal and to ask for and provide support is helpful, necessary and beneficial for human interaction.

Chapter 3

Ten keys to a successful staff support group

David Kennard and Phil Hartley

This chapter summarises what, in the experience of the authors and other facilitators of staff support groups, have been found to be the important ingredients for a successful staff support group. Many of these will be addressed in more detail in the chapters that follow.

1 The request or proposal for a staff support group is based on realistic and agreed expectations

Before the facilitator sets foot in the group room, he or she needs to make sure that the group will be built on solid ground, not on a swamp or the side of a volcano. To go from metaphor to everyday reality, there may be various reasons why a staff support group is requested or proposed, and the would-be facilitator should be on the lookout for conflicts of interests or hidden agendas. We go into these in more detail in Chapter 4. Here we will highlight the factors that, so far as the facilitator is able to judge them from preliminary contacts, will provide reasonable assurance of solid ground.

- Staff morale is reasonably good. A team with very low morale is likely to avoid the group as too painful, or to load it with unrealistic expectations.
- The expectations of what the group can achieve are clear and realistic. The group is not being proposed to deal with a problem that actually requires a different kind of intervention – e.g. management changes, better procedures for clinical decision-making, help with a troubled member of the team.
- Different subgroups or levels within the organisation may have different or conflicting views about a staff support group. If the group is for a team that is part of a larger organisation, the facilitator clarifies that there is support for the group at both the team and higher level, as opposition at either level can undermine the group.
- Bolton and Roberts (1994: 157) suggest that the overt, stated aims of a staff group may not be the whole story and that there may also be

covert aims – known to a few but not to everyone – or unconscious aims that only become apparent as the group progresses. The facilitator does their best to discover and bring into the open any covert aims of individuals or subgroups. Unconscious aims may be harder to identify in advance.

- If the organisation has had experience of previous staff groups or facilitators, the facilitator is able to discuss how these colour present expectations.
- The facilitator is comfortable with and feels able to support the aims of the organisation, and is satisfied that the aims of the group will not be at odds with the aims and values of the organisation. This may be particularly relevant if, for example, a liberal-minded facilitator is asked to lead a staff support group in a secure facility with a strong ethos of control.

2 The facilitator sets up the group with clarity, transparency and full staff involvement

Assuming the facilitator and the team/organisation decide together to go ahead and set up the group, the early stages will be vital to giving the group a good start. To use the ground metaphor again, this is equivalent, having once checked the ground is solid, to building firm foundations.

- Senior staff and managers make known their support for setting up the group. Denial of the need for support in senior staff makes it unlikely the staff support group will succeed.
- It is agreed who will and won't be eligible to attend – for example, whether the group is only for permanent qualified members of the team, or will include students, temporary staff, administrative staff, etc. The question of whether or not to include senior staff and managers is a difficult one – both ways have advantages and disadvantages (see Chapter 4).
- The aims are clearly stated in the group in order to minimise confusion or uncertainty, and the potential benefits of the group are described in terms that all the staff can agree with. A group that has the approval of only a subgroup of the staff team will not get off to a good start.
- Members are able to discuss what they hope to get from the group and any concerns they have about it. Reluctance to attend because of the disruption caused to work schedules, doubts about the value of the group, anxieties about being put on the spot, etc., are acknowledged and dealt with at face value rather than being interpreted as underlying resistance to the group.
- The facilitator is open about any discussions that have taken place with management about the group.

- There is discussion about any previous experience staff members have had of support groups and how this has coloured their expectations.

3 There is mutual agreement on the choice of facilitator

- The team is involved in the choice of the group facilitator or in confirming the choice if it is made by senior staff or managers in the first instance. To do this they need to have some idea about what approach they are looking for.
- The facilitator is seen as neutral in terms of their relationship with the organisation. Either they are external to the organisation or, if they work in the organisation, the connection is not seen as one that will prejudice their views on issues discussed in the group. (See Chapters 11 and 13 for examples of issues faced by internal facilitators.)
- The facilitator for their part feels they can work with this staff team – that there is sufficient common ground.

4 Room and time arrangements are appropriate

The organisational arrangements for the group are important, both in practical terms and for the message they convey about the status of the group.

- The group meets in the same room each time, rather than being moved around because of other priorities. The room is big enough to have space for a circle where everyone can see each other, with easily moved chairs that can accommodate however many come to a session. The room is free from outside noise, interruption or being overlooked.
- The meetings last for at least an hour and are held regularly – weekly, fortnightly or monthly. Less frequent meetings last for longer – one and a half or two hours.
- Arrangements are made for cover to enable as many staff as possible to attend the meetings.
- The numbers attending meetings are anticipated to be between a minimum of 5 and a maximum of 15–20. Fewer than 5 makes it hard to get interaction going, more than 15–20 can make participating feel daunting – though this will depend to an extent on the group experience of the members. (See below on very low attendance.)

5 A sense of safety is established and maintained

Once the group is under way, safety is the initial priority. It is important, indeed vital, to the group's success that members feel the atmosphere and the format are safe enough to take part in. For individuals unfamiliar with discussing their experiences in a group the situation may feel like being parachuted into a jungle with risks and dangers all around. There are some things that will help the group feel safer – many of these come under the heading of the group's 'boundaries'.

- Time and duration: members know when the group starts and ends and can plan their other commitments accordingly.
- Attendance: in our experience it generally works best if attendance is voluntary but that the purpose of the group is seen as giving support as well as receiving it, so members don't think they should only attend when they have a problem. Compulsory attendance is not recommended because it is unenforceable, and will produce its own problems if members feel they are attending against their will.
- Time keeping: over time members learn the importance of attending on time and staying for the duration of the session, as indicators of respect for and sensitivity to each other's needs.
- If attendance falls to a very low level it is important to address this. Members can be asked to take responsibility for trying to increase attendance by advertising the group and finding out reasons why people aren't coming. If the problem persists the facilitator may set a minimum number, below which they will not continue the meeting.
- Confidentiality: ground rules are agreed that what is discussed in the group is not talked about outside the group. There also needs to be agreement about how an issue raised in the group that does need to be taken somewhere else is dealt with.
- Topics that are 'off limits': members need to be sure that their privacy will not be invaded and that the group will not venture into areas that undermine the capacity of colleagues to work together. As Lederberg (1998: 276) points out, 'the demands of the work setting dictate some suppression of feelings, and the support group must not probe them except where they are toxic to individuals and task'.

6 The facilitator's style and technique are appropriate to the needs of the group

There is a consensus among writers on staff support groups that the facilitator's intervention style must be different from conducting a therapeutic group or an experiential group. We would also argue that it should be different from a sensitivity group, as the staff are coming to a staff support group to help them do their job with less stress or emotional discomfort, but they have not necessarily come to learn more about themselves or about team dynamics, although this may happen. If the facilitator is also a group therapist the distinction may take some self-discipline to maintain. The following are some of the key points made by Lederberg (1998), Rifkind (1995) and Milton and Davison (1997).

- The facilitator maintains an adult-to-adult style of communication with the members, avoiding the use of interpretations or therapeutic terms that imply a detached or analytic attitude towards the group, generally being more 'real', more themselves, than they would if conducting a therapeutic group. The facilitator may be aware of unconscious staff motivations or transference reactions but almost never interprets these.
- He or she may open each session with a simple prompt asking how the week has been – which makes it a different experience from the silence that may open a therapy or experiential group.
- The facilitator doesn't allow anxiety or regression to develop, in contrast to a therapeutic or experiential group where they would be seen as an important part of the group process.
- The facilitator may use a discussion of clinical material or institutional events to introduce some psychological learning, but is careful about using events in the group in this way in case this is felt to be intrusive.
- Confrontation between members is 'cautiously supported' – and modulated to encourage a constructive outcome, as the priority is that the group remains safe.

7 The group deals with important issues

Feeling safe is the top priority, certainly to begin with, but if the group maintains its safety at the cost of not discussing anything of importance, members may begin to wonder what the point of the group is. Getting the balance right between safety and dealing with important topics is what taxes the skill and judgement of the facilitator. Some of the important issues that a staff support group may deal with include the following.

- Sharing, and normalising, shameful, guilty or angry reactions staff may have towards difficult patients, residents or clients.
- Acknowledging and accepting feelings of vulnerability, failure or not coping.
- Discussing obstacles to team working.
- Exploring difficult ethical and existential questions – for example, a seriously ill or disabled patient's wish to die, or the injustice of human suffering.

Rifkind has a concise way of referring to the shifting nature of what is important in a staff consultation group (her use of this term is quite close to our idea of a staff support group). She says that the function of the consultant (facilitator in our terms) is to help the team identify 'where the tension point might be, and what they might be able to do about it' (Rifkind 1995: 220). She identifies one of the important issues as an organisational one – to help the group to 'understand the structures that exist, how decisions are made, where power lies and what potential they have to influence things' (Rifkind 1995: 221).

8 The facilitator helps the group stay 'on task'

One of the facilitator's main functions is continually to monitor whether the group is 'on task' or avoiding important issues. Groups can wander off the point in various ways, some more obvious than others.

- Gossiping.
- Avoiding discussing the client group at all – treating the group as 'time out' from work.
- Losing flexibility – getting fixed on one topic or issue.
- The group being 'co-opted' by one or two members with a grievance, to support their cause.

Given the flexibility of staff support groups it may sometimes be difficult to judge when the group has gone 'off task' – e.g. if light hearted banter between members has gone past the point of being a warm up to more meaningful communication, or if discussion of a particular problem has become repetitive and non-productive. The facilitator can be helped by bearing in mind that 'support is needed to enable staff to face rather than evade difficult issues' (Bolton and Roberts 1994: 164) and, to repeat our use of Rifkind's note, that the function of the consultant is to help the team identify where the tension point might be.

9 The facilitator is aware of his or her own responses and takes care not to let them interfere with their role

Facilitating a staff support group exposes the facilitator to a wide range of psychological impacts, depending on the nature of the team's work. These may cloud their judgement and make strong demands on the facilitator's own resources and self-awareness. Facilitators also have their own needs – to feel wanted, appreciated, competent, effective – and need to be aware of and manage these needs so that they don't interfere with how they carry out their role.

- In units dealing with life threatening conditions (e.g. intensive care units, hospices) there are what Lederberg (1998: 278) calls the 'raw issues of hope, fear, pain, loss, death', where 'facilitators must draw on their own inner resources to cope with immediacy and volume of human tragedies.'

- In settings where the work of the team may be viewed ambivalently or with hostility by their clients (e.g. prisons or secure units, services for people with personality disorders), the team may transmit some of the negative feelings they experience on to the staff support group and the facilitator – who has to cope with and try to understand the source of feeling mistrusted, useless, rejected or dangerous.
- Similarly with other responses – e.g. impatience, boredom, feeling exploited, feeling competitive with the unit leader – the facilitator must keep a careful watch on his or her own reactions and try to use them to understand the processes that may be impacting on the staff. The facilitator may find they have their own strong reactions to institutional processes that are affecting the staff. Lederberg (1998) points out that the facilitator should not let their own reactions to the stresses of job uncertainty and organisational changes lead to a defeatist climate in the group.
- Bolton and Roberts conclude their review of staff support groups as follows:

> The pull towards getting caught up in unconscious group and institutional processes, using the group to meet one's own needs rather than to further the task for which the group exists, is universal. Only if the consultants can disentangle themselves sufficiently from these processes to think, be aware of their failing without too much guilt or need to blame others, and maintain a reflective attitude towards their own feelings and behaviour as well as towards the experience of the group members, can the group develop a similarly thoughtful, non-judgemental, self-scanning stance.
>
> (Bolton and Roberts 1994: 165)

Facilitating a staff support group is no less demanding, and in some ways more so, than conducting a therapeutic group. For all the above reasons the success of a staff support group may depend on, and will certainly be helped by, the facilitator establishing their own external supervision or consultancy to help them understand and make use of their reactions to the group.

10 There are arrangements for monitoring the group's success in meeting the needs of members and the organisation

There is agreement at or near the start of the group on the expectations of the organisation for the group, and on aims agreed with the members (points 1 and 2 pp. 26–28). There also needs to be a decision on how and to whom the facilitator is accountable for their work and for reviewing the group's continuation. This may be with the head of the organisation, the team leader, the staff team as a whole, or some combination of these.

Just as the facilitator monitors the flow of conversation in the group for its relevance to the members' day-to-day work, so the group needs to be monitored to check that it is continuing to meet the needs and expectations of the organisation and the staff members. How this is done depends partly on who the facilitator is accountable to, but is best done outside the usual group meetings to avoid the result being biased by the most vocal members. There are a number of possibilities:

- the simplest – monitoring attendance – is also one of the best indicators;
- a periodic meeting between the facilitator and unit/team leader for mutual feedback within the agreed limits of confidentiality;
- an anonymous evaluation questionnaire completed by all staff;
- an independent person asking staff for their views of the group.

The position of the group in the organisation is also reflected in how the group is described and evaluated in unit documentation (e.g. staff hand-outs, written policies and objectives), and it is useful for the facilitator to be aware of and contribute to these.

SUMMARY

This chapter has outlined the requirements for setting up and running a staff support group that, taken together, will determine its outcome. It also highlights the amount of thought and care that go into a successful group, and why it is so easy for a group to flounder or fail. The chapters that follow unpack these requirements in more detail.

Chapter 4

Setting up a staff support group

Phil Hartley and David Kennard

This chapter considers the starting point for setting up a group from two perspectives – the team's and the facilitator's – and then considers the questions and steps involved in deciding whether and how to go ahead.

FROM THE PERSPECTIVE OF THE TEAM OR INDIVIDUAL SEEKING A FACILITATOR – HOW TO APPROACH A FACILITATOR

There are a number of questions it is helpful to consider before approaching a staff support group facilitator.

- Why is a staff support group needed?
- Is it part of a staff support strategy, or in response to a particular issue?
- If it is in response to a particular issue, why now, rather than the last issue? What has tipped the balance to need a staff support group?
- What are the aims of a group?
- Consider the logistics of where and when the group can meet and how shift workers may attend?
- Who should approach a potential facilitator?
- What is the means of approaching them?

It is helpful if these questions are thought about by the team that the group is intended for. It helps to consult with people and involve them in the process. It is not uncommon for senior staff to have the idea for a staff support group and not discuss it at all, or not sufficiently with staff. By involving the staff in thinking about the questions posed, the first meeting with the facilitator will not be characterised by bewilderment and resentment.

Why is a staff support group needed?

There are likely to be different opinions about whether a group is needed. At this stage it is desirable, but not essential, that there is a consensus about the idea of a group. Whether a group is wanted can be finally decided after meeting with a facilitator. The most fundamental issue is whether the staff want to sit down with one another and discuss the issue they have identified and their reaction to it.

Is it part of a staff support strategy?

In a new service or team, a staff support group can be organised as part of the service planning and operation. Most of the questions posed in this section still apply. The essential difference is that new staff come into an existing group and staff support is part of the culture and is normal. Setting up a new group in an existing service often means changing its culture and is likely to be met with more resistance and anxiety.

If it is in response to a particular issue, why now?

This question faces the team with thinking about the more unconscious reasons for wanting a staff support group. The usual answer is that an accumulation of events has left the staff feeling in need of support, or that a particularly serious event has occurred. This may be the case, and further thought is not necessary. But teams usually deal with difficult situations as part of their normal practice, and the question *why now?* can reveal an unspoken issue. It may be a significant staff member leaving, internal conflict, organisation change, or a senior staff member (often a manager) struggling and feeling out of control. The team may not find the answer to 'why now?', but posing the question helps them to slow down and reflect on their dynamics, something that is usually impossible to do as part of a rushed daily routine.

What are the main aims of the group?

Obviously the answer to 'why now?' influences the aims. It is helpful to be as clear as possible what the team want from a group, and whether they are prepared to discuss in the staff support group how they work together. Most teams find the reality of discussing their work, and their professional relationships, anxiety provoking.

Logistics

Participating in a staff support group in a busy service is difficult, particularly when staff work shifts. The more the team can consider where and when to meet the better. It may not be possible to run the group away from the unit, or to guarantee that there will not be interruptions, but in order for the group to feel sufficiently safe, privacy and regular attendance are essential. Some staff can only attend if they also feel able to leave the group and attend to a situation. This is mostly likely in clinical services when staffing numbers are low. The more staff can think about the logistics of privacy and attendance, in conjunction with managers, the more likely it is that people will be able to attend regularly and punctually in an appropriate setting. Discussing this with managers includes them in decisions about the impact of the group on organisational practice and vice versa, so lodging the group more firmly in the organisation's consciousness. This makes the group more likely to be a space that is protected and respected.

The room used for a staff support group should be large enough for the number of people attending, and should be available on a consistent basis. The proposed membership should consider minimum and maximum numbers that can attend. This will usually involve thinking about who attends. This will be discussed in more detail in due course. The minimum number for a viable group is probably 4 or 5 members, with a maximum of between 10 and 20 (Haig 2000: 315). In our experience, groups of 6 to 15 people are an average and manageable number. The room should be spacious enough to allow the membership to sit in a circle and not around a table, which is too formal and reminiscent of other meetings.

Who should approach the facilitator and how?

Setting up a staff support group involves logistical and financial negotiation and decisions. Senior staff are responsible for these or have access to decision-making structures, so it is more practical that they approach the facilitator. If the staff member has direct contact with the team or service that the group is for, so much the better. Junior staff can make the initial contact, but are likely to be a conduit to meeting senior staff. There are various ways that approaches can be made. In our experience it is often through a personal contact. The numbers of people facilitating staff groups are few, and often they are group analysts, psychotherapists or clinical tutors who are known to be interested in such work.

Alternatively, facilitators can be reached through adverts in professional journals, newsletters, websites, or email lists of members of relevant organisations. These often request the facilitator to make contact and may involve them being selected by a recruitment or interview process. If this is the case the team can be involved in writing the advert, job description, person specification and interview questions. This process can help distil down what a team if looking for in their facilitator. The team can be involved in interviewing the facilitator, which is inclusive and democratic.

FROM THE PERSPECTIVE OF THE FACILITATOR

Responding to the initial contact

The facilitation of a staff support group starts with the initial contact made with the facilitator. The successful establishment of a helpful group is made more likely by an active and questioning approach at this early stage. Various authors (Bram and Katz 1989; Lederberg 1998) and our own experience suggest that the usual method of getting support at work is through relationships with colleagues. The enquiry or request for a staff support group is therefore unusual, and may indicate that the usual coping strategies are not working well enough. That may be a team's experience, perhaps after a particular trauma or period of change, or it may be a perception by an individual member that is not shared by the team. Alternatively the request for a staff support group may be part of a new team's service structure, and be wanted to help them achieve their primary task.

Questions the facilitator needs to consider include the following.

- What is the relationship between the person making the request and the team?
- At what level in the team, service or organisation does that person operate?
- Why is the person making the approach?

These questions form the basis of a hypothesis about the function of the group that can be tested as the process unfolds.

What is the relationship between the person making the request and the team?

In our experience, the person who first contacts the potential facilitator is usually someone who is comfortable with the idea of a staff support group. They are more likely to know who might have the skills and experience to facilitate a group. If not, they are aware of organisations and networks that facilitators may be members of. This is more likely to set them apart from the team in some way – e.g. a trainee helpfully offering to advertise the request in their training organisation's literature or website. The implicit message is that they know more about the subject than other team members. The facilitator should consider what position that places them in once the approach has been made. Will they be seen as an ally of whoever has approached them? A different situation is where a team has asked their manager to commission a staff support group and approach potential facilitators. The facilitator has to untangle why the request is from a manager of the service and not from the member who initiated it, and how the manager may 'translate' the team's request. Do they communicate the request exactly, or interpret it, conveying their own perceptions and reasons for a staff support group.

At what level in the team, service or organisation does that person operate?

Example

A junior member of a team approached a potential facilitator to facilitate a new staff support group. The staff member was part of a team being led in new and challenging directions. Although senior staff were apparently aware of the approach and gave tacit agreement to a group being set up, they did not participate in feasibility and planning meetings. When the group started, senior members of the team did not attend.

Junior members were angry about the new clinical direction they were being led in. They felt hurt and rejected by their managers and the organisation, and that their previous work was unappreciated. The request for a staff support group represented a wish to air their dissatisfaction and to be heard by managers. The lack of involvement of senior figures merely perpetuated team divisions and conflict.

In this example the facilitator has to consider why, when senior staff are leading a new clinical strategy, that it is a junior staff member who is left to contact the facilitator and what that may suggest about team dynamics. The absence of senior staff approaching the facilitator was predictive that they would not be attending the staff support group. This was probably to avoid the difficult feelings being expressed by the team. Had the approach been by someone leading the new strategy, the facilitator might wonder whether the manager needed the facilitator to help push through changes. More benignly an approach by a manager in this example could be out of concern about the impact of change on the team. In this case it is more likely a manager will attend the group. Group membership will be discussed in more detail later in this chapter.

Why is the person making the approach?

Why you? and *why now?* are common thoughts or questions that clinicians think and ask when they try to understand someone's difficulties and what triggered them. The same questions are relevant when being asked to set up a staff support group.

Having thought about who makes the approach and their position in the hierarchy, it is helpful to think why it is that individual in particular. Have they been asked or have they volunteered? In the example of the team asking their manager to approach a facilitator, it was because they needed both the manager and the potential facilitator to know they did not feel well enough looked after.

Someone, or a subgroup of workers, that is seen as troubled or 'troublesome' at work, and that wants a staff support group, may be asked to go and explore its viability. This is most likely after a period of vociferous dissatisfaction and requests for additional support. The request to 'go and explore its viability' is likely to represent a desire to shut them up and get rid of the problem, with no real intention to support them.

The facilitator's hypothesis should consider both the manifest and latent reasons for the request. The manifest rationale will, of course, include why the request is being made. The reason will usually be to support the primary task of the organisation or service. The facilitator will need to 'do the homework necessary to understand the institutional mission and the ways in which the institution is organised to carry it out' (Lederberg 1998: 278). The facilitator is not just wondering what is behind the request and the approach of the individual, but also the organisational structure and context. The impact an organisation has on a team can help or hinder its ability to perform its task. A request for a staff group may be in response to the team's relationship and experience of the wider organisation. The ability of a staff support group to influence an organisation is limited, unless the facilitator negotiates contact with senior members of the organisation as part of the process of setting up a group.

Example

A client seriously assaults another client causing significant physical injury. Some staff are injured while intervening. The assault occurs in an inpatient residential facility and is categorised as a serious untoward incident. The subsequent enquiry identifies several areas of concern and makes recommendations to change procedures and practice. A senior manager who was not directly involved in the incident, but has responsibility for the unit, is concerned that the staff are burnt out and traumatised. This manager requests a suitably experienced organisation to set up a staff support group. The facilitator meets the manager and describes him as a concrete thinker who likes practical solutions. During the discussion, it transpires that there is no suitable venue for a group to meet on the unit. The shift pattern will make attendance extremely difficult and the manager will not be attending the group. He is difficult to engage in discussing logistical solutions, preferring to delegate to more junior managers who are not aware of the initiative.

Hypotheses

In this example the facilitator had several potential hypotheses.

- The staff support group was being requested because of the senior manager's anxiety about the contributing factors leading up to the serious untoward incident. The request was being driven by the manager's anxiety and not the team's. The lack of interest in discussing logistical solutions and desire not to attend may indicate a culture of blame by managers and ineffective leadership.
- A culture of blame, and lack of leadership, coupled with no consultation about the group, may make staff anxious and suspicious about the aim of the group. Will the facilitator be seen as part of 'the management', as someone who will be critical and unhelpful? The lack of consultation with junior staff may suggest anxiety about facing how they really feel about their work and the incident.
- A staff support group may leave staff feeling even more inadequate and damaged. In an organisation whose culture and practice is often reactive and fire fighting, rather than considered and planned, staff rely on having to survive. To consider how close they are to not surviving can leave them less defended and less able to cope with their work. (Haigh cautions against staff groups being 'wrongly seen as a panacea for problems they are not designed to address' (Haigh 2000: 314).)
- In this example the facilitator may be just the person the staff are looking for to take out their feelings on. The odds are against this group working, and the facilitator is likely to be blamed by the manager for not making the staff feel better. The manager has found someone to take his place. Bramley cautions that when setting up sensitivity groups the facilitator is 'a sitting target for organisational paranoia, idealisation (with its underside of contempt), and projections of all kinds' (Bramley 1990: 315).

DECIDING WHETHER TO FACILITATE A STAFF SUPPORT GROUP

Much depends on whether the facilitator, having been approached and thought about the possible reasons a group is wanted, thinks it will work. This will partly depend on the facilitator's view on their own ability to manage the potential difficulties. Setting up a new group requires a long-term commitment and significant capacity not to be overly disillusioned by poor attendance, anxiety and even hostility. Tentative discussions with the person who has made the approach can be a helpful indicator of a willingness to think about underlying team dynamics. In our experience, if the logistical problems and underlying reasons for setting up a group are not overwhelming then it should go ahead. A barometer of this is the effort the commissioner puts into managing the logistics, and the feel of the conversation – how flexible they are and receptive to ideas.

Before finally agreeing to facilitate a group it is helpful to ask to meet with the whole team to discuss it further.

MEETING THE TEAM

Meeting the team to discuss the idea may take a few sessions (though meeting more than two or three times risks these meetings about the 'idea' becoming the group itself). Key questions to discuss at this stage include the following.

- Do they know about the initiative and are they interested?
- What are the group's aims?
- Have they had a group before?
- Negotiating logistics and ground rules.
- Discussing who will attend and how the group will work.

Meeting the staff gives an indication of the viability of a group, indicated by the number that attend, whether apologies are sent, and the room that is used. Poorly attended and badly organised meetings at this stage are a poor prognostic indicator, but not necessarily a reason not to go ahead.

Do they know about the initiative and are they interested?

It is surprising how often staff are not aware that a manager has proposed a group, or are only told because they are being asked to attend a meeting with the facilitator, who then is left to inform them and manage their reactions.

Examples
A facilitator was approached by a manager to support a team who were struggling to work with personality disorder. On meeting the team the facilitator discovered they knew nothing of their manager's opinion about their clinical struggles. The request said much more about the relationship between the team and their manager. However, once recognized and spoken about, over time it became a highly valued group that could discuss their experience of being managed.

An example of good consultation about a group was staff being surveyed about the idea and putting forward their suggestions about a group. When the facilitator met with them, the fact they had been consulted with was obvious. However, the people attending the meeting had different ideas about what they wanted from a group from those who had responded to the survey, and this resulted in the facilitator re-negotiating the aims with them despite the work supposedly achieved by the survey. This illustrated a senior/junior staff split about clinical developments the group was supposed to support them with.

What are the group's aims?

The commissioner of a staff support group, even with good consultation with a team, can be surprised by what people say they want from a group when meeting a facilitator. Apart from the inconsistencies of human inter-action, this is also explained by staff saying different things to facilitators and managers. It is crucial that the facilitator and proposed group members know and agree the aims face-to-face, because they dictate the relevance of the group to people, and how it will be used.

An aim may be 'to discuss how we are affected by our work'. This may seem uncontroversial, but is likely to be anxiety provoking and raise structural questions. Staff will be anxious about 'who feels what' and whether they can admit to their feelings. People in new groups in particular, but even in longstanding groups, can struggle to know what to say. People often state they do not have anything to talk about this week. Staff's anxieties about disclosing their feelings can be focused on structural issues about how to use the group, like asking about a rota system to ensure everyone gets a chance to say something. Given the degree of anxiety about disclosing feelings in front of colleagues and the inevitable anxiety about team dynamics, the aims have to include being able to discuss this or it cannot be worked with. This should be explained to the people attending the meeting. People are usually accepting of this rationale, but with reser-vations that it will be anxiety provoking and even threatening.

The aims have to reflect the different needs of people attending the group, including senior staff, junior staff and the facilitator.

Have they had a group before?

In the above example of good consultation with a team, the facilitator did not know until meeting them that there was a significant history of failed groups. Discussing this with the staff allowed some exploration of why they had failed and what could be done differently. The facilitator not being advised of this formed part of the hypothesis about the senior and junior staff split and how much in touch with one another they were. Whatever the team's previous experiences of a group are, they set up an expectation and dynamic about how a group will be.

Negotiating logistics and ground rules

If the logistics have already been agreed, namely time, venue and frequency, it is as well to clarify with all present. If decisions have not been reached, discussing them with everyone involves them in the decision-making.

Ground rules are important, as they set up expectations, manage anxiety and ultimately keep the group safe. They will usually include the following.

- Punctuality – starting and ending the group.
- Sending apologies if someone cannot attend.
- Whether attendance is expected or not. In our experience this is a commonly raised question by staff. Our view is that obligatory attendance is counter-productive, rather there should be a culture of attendance as a priority that is set by example.
- Limits of confidentiality. Most groups have a confidentiality rule that anything discussed in the group remains in the group. This is not always practical or desirable. All staff, including the facilitator, have responsibilities to report issues of concern about risks to staff or others or gross professional misconduct. It is crucial this is spelt out and that a decision to breach confidentiality would be usually discussed in the group first.

Who will attend?

Who will attend the group is often a contentious issue. Haigh (2000: 315) says groups should be 'trans-professional'. This is usually the case in clinical services and most people do not object to the multi-disciplinary team members attending. Despite this, doctors often do not attend and do not feel the need to. Given their role, and position in the hierarchy, this is unhelpful, but is often an insurmountable problem.

There may be debate about who the team consists of. Does it include temporary workers, trainees, students etc? Are clinical and domestic staff all part of the team? The facilitator can help the thinking by asking what is lost if one subgroup or another does not attend.

Staff can be particularly worried about managers attending staff groups, as can managers. Staff worry about feeling silenced and judged, managers about being vulnerable and attacked. Whatever is agreed there are pros and cons. We think that, though more complicated, it is better for all staff of whatever discipline and position in the hierarchy to attend if possible. Some of the pros and cons are as follows.

Pros:
- an integrative experience;
- universality of experience;
- deeper understanding of one another;
- flattened hierarchy in the session;
- senior staff attendance promotes the group as 'valuable'.

Cons:
- team splits/conflicts can be unmanageable;
- the team cannot bear to understand one another's experience e.g. a manager cannot tolerate junior staff members' distress;
- junior and senior staff feel exposed and vulnerable in front of one another.

How will the group work?

Staff are interested in how the group will work and how the facilitator will deal with things. Commonly asked questions include the following.

- Will poor attendance close the group?
- Will there be long silences?
- What happens if people get upset?
- What will we talk about?
- Do we have to attend?
- Will managers be coming?
- Can we leave the group to deal with a crisis?
- Will there be a review of the group?
- Will I be analysed?

Such questions are legitimate and practical answers go a long way to giving staff the information to decide whether they want a group and whether they trust the facilitator enough to proceed. Questions should be answered directly, and not interpreted as hiding an underlying anxiety. It can be helpful to discuss with the group what they think the answer should be and for the facilitator to be a source of information about the relative advantages and disadvantages about a particular issue. For example, what if someone gets upset? Most people attending the meeting would want to support someone in distress and not provoke upset. In reality, there can often be a temporary drop in attendance if someone is openly distressed. At this early stage, it is helpful to suggest that someone who is upset is supported and that this may best be done by people discussing situations that have affected them similarly.

The questions raised here, and how to respond to them, will be discussed in more detail in Chapter 6 on ways of responding to common problems.

The purpose of meeting the staff is to inform them of what a group is like and how the facilitator will work. It is a chance for the facilitator to finally decide whether to do the group or not. If the answer is 'yes' by all parties, the next stage is a written communication or contract.

The contract

There may need to be two contracts, one between the facilitator and the organisation, and one between the facilitator and the group, the usual difference being that the first may include information about fees. Negotiating the fee is an arrangement between the facilitator and the commissioner. The level of fee depends on the experience and seniority of the facilitator and what the market determines.

The contract between the facilitator and the group members specifies the aims, time, venue, and ground rules of the group and other relevant information from the meetings with the staff, including an agreed start date and any reviews. Group members will often advocate using a notice board or staff communication book for this contract. In our experience many people do not read these, and a letter to all staff from the facilitator creates a personal relationship and reliable form of communication. If most staff have attended the meeting this information can be conveyed verbally.

This personal communication summarises an essential function of the preliminary meetings described in this chapter in that it reinforces the individual relationship the facilitator must have with each team member as well as the whole group. A successful group is one in which each person feels listened to and their views validated by the facilitator. The contract represents an agreement on how the team will work together with one another and with the facilitator. The role of the facilitator is the subject of our next chapter.

Chapter 5

The role of the facilitator

David Kennard and Phil Hartley

Even when a contract has spelled out the agreed aims and ground rules of the group, the role of the facilitator in a staff support group is more ambiguous and harder to define than in other kinds of group. There are good reasons for this. In groups where membership changes from session to session continuity and consistency are harder to achieve. The needs of the group and the appropriate style of facilitation may also change from one session to the next. The flexibility that is a strength of staff support groups, as we described in Chapter 1, also introduces more possibilities for the facilitator's role. And there is an important element in the role of the facilitator that is outside the group itself, and has to do with the meaning of the group's existence and survival for staff and for the organisation.

Having made these caveats, we will try to set out what we see as the core elements of the facilitator's role in a staff support group, putting them under the following headings:

- broad components of the role;
- the early sessions;
- boundary maintenance;
- task maintenance;
- types of intervention;
- working with feelings;
- surviving.

BROAD COMPONENTS OF THE ROLE

To the extent that a staff support group is a group that aims to help its members talk about experiences that have a personal and emotional impact, the facilitator's role has certain elements that are shared with all groups with this aim, including therapeutic groups. Yalom, a doyen of group therapists, writes that, 'the basic posture of the therapist to a patient

Box 5.1 Therapeutic factors in groups – adapted from Yalom (1985)

Catharsis: emotional release leading to relief – includes ventilation of feelings either positive or negative about life events or other group members.

Self-disclosure: the act of revealing personal information to the group.

Learning from interpersonal actions: the attempt to relate constructively and adaptively within the group, by initiating some behaviour or responding to other group members. More important than others members' reactions is the individual's effort to relate constructively.

Universality: the individual perceives that other group members have similar problems and feelings and this reduces the sense of uniqueness.

Acceptance: the individual has a sense of belonging, being supported, cared for and valued by the group, and of being accepted by others even when revealing something about themselves they had regarded as unacceptable.

Altruism: the person feels better about themselves or learns something positive about themselves through helping other group members.

Guidance: the individual receives useful, factual information or explicit advice and suggestions from the group.

Self-understanding: the person learns something important about their behaviour, assumptions, motivation or unconscious thoughts.

Vicarious learning: the individual experiences something of value for themselves through the observation of other group members.

Instillation of hope: the individual gains a sense of optimism about their own progress or potential for progress in the group.

must be one of concern, acceptance, genuineness, empathy. Nothing, no technical considerations, takes precedence over this.' (Yalom 1985: 112). This applies no less to the staff support group facilitator. We would add that the basic posture should include a genuine interest in the experiences of the staff – as against promoting a particular model of care – and real respect for the efforts the staff are making to carry out difficult tasks.

Yalom has identified a number of 'therapeutic factors' that occur in groups, which it is the task of the group therapist to promote (Yalom 1985). These are shown in Box 5.1.

While stressing that support groups are not therapeutic groups, it seems to us that many of these factors are generally beneficial elements in any helping group. For example, staff are able to recognize similarities between their own experiences and those of other group members and consequently feel less alone (Olofsson 2005) – the benefit of universality. They may reveal something that they fear will make them seem unfit for the job, and be relieved to find they are still accepted by their colleagues – Wojciechowska opens Chapter 12 with a dramatic example of the importance of such acceptance. They may be able to understand better their own reactions to clients or situations – Humphreys describes the complex process leading to self-understanding in Chapter 13. They may use the group cathartically to express their feelings after a traumatic or painful experience, and new or junior staff may get helpful guidance from more experienced colleagues on how to manage a tricky situation.

It is important that the facilitator is careful to avoid the group becoming a place for personal therapy for its members, even if some members seem to wish this, for this is not the contract of the staff support group and other members may soon stop coming. However, there is every reason to encourage the beneficial human experiences that are potentially present in any group.

THE EARLY SESSIONS

Following the initial meetings to flesh out the agreement for a staff support group, the group will get underway with a mixture of hopes and fears. The role of the facilitator at this stage involves reducing the inevitable anxiety about how things will go, helping members to talk (but not too much or going too deep early on), and helping the group to work on its agreed aims.

Reducing anxiety

It is natural for everyone including the facilitator to be anxious in the early stages. As a general rule of thumb, the greater the anxiety the less helpful are long silences and the more helpful is a certain amount of guidance or direction to structure the discussion. Low-key modelling of openness can be helpful, like 'I guess we're all bound to feel a bit anxious at the moment, and I'm no exception.' Simple suggestions for structure include asking if anyone has anything they'd like to bring up, or suggesting members to go round each saying how they are feeling at the moment or what sort of day they are having. The aim is not to produce pearls of wisdom but to help people begin to settle down and feel more comfortable. Hearing other people echoing one's own thoughts or experience generally helps in this respect.

Helping members to talk (but not too much or going too deep at first)

Not everyone is a talker and the facilitator needs to allow for this. People feel their way into group situations in different ways – some prefer to watch and listen, to benefit for 'vicarious learning', others jump in with both feet. Facilitating comments like those above or, if someone has ventured to bring something up, asking 'what do other people think?' or 'has that been other people's experience?' can help to get the ball rolling. The extremes to try to avoid are lots of silence or letting one member monopolise the group.

The former raises too much anxiety in a new group and the latter discourages interaction and may act as a screen for the rest of the group to hide behind. Depth is also an issue – someone making a big personal disclosure is likely to scare the rest of the group, who will wonder if they are expected to go next. It may also worry the discloser if they had not intended to say so much so soon. The facilitator has a role of both encouraging enough disclosure to make the group feel meaningful but not so much that it feels unsafe.

Helping the group to work on the agreed aims

If the group has agreed on certain aims, one of the ways the facilitator can open the session is to remind the group of these. It is possible that these aims will have been phrased in fairly general terms – e.g. to explore difficult situations in the workplace; to support each other in coping with stressful situations; to challenge stereotypes that impair team working. Translating these into practice may not be straightforward, and the role of facilitator is to help the group think about how to address these aims and what obstacles may have to be overcome first – such as learning to be comfortable with open discussion in the group.

BOUNDARY MAINTENANCE

While the group is evolving and the members are getting used to meeting together, the facilitator also needs to keep an eye on behaviour and events that whittle away the boundaries of the group, and could if unchecked begin to undermine its ability to fulfil its purpose. The key boundaries are those of time – when the group starts and ends – and place – where the group meets. If either of these start to change from meeting to meeting, the group will soon cease to be a reliable place to meet for support and will start to resemble all the other things that get pushed around by the pressures of the day. Challenges to these boundaries can come from both within and outside the group.

Boundary challenges from within the group

In the early stages individuals may test the time boundaries of the group by coming late, leaving early, allowing themselves to be called out, taking phone calls in the group, etc. The facilitator should try to respond with tactful firmness, reminding people what was agreed, being understanding of the pressures on staff but pointing out that such actions by an individual impact on everyone else in the group – e.g. waiting for the group to start, or not being sure when it will end, or conversations having to stop midway. It is important (and sometimes difficult) not to appear critical or hostile towards an individual, since this can increase other members' anxiety about criticism, but to focus the remarks on what is in the best interests of the group and its aims.

Boundary challenges from outside the group

Another threat to the group in the early stages may be attempts to move it if there is pressure on room space, or to cancel it because of a staffing crisis. This calls for the facilitator to make enquiries as to the reasons and if necessary to contact the person in the organisation with whom he has a written contract, to reinforce the importance of consistency if staff are to develop confidence in the group, and also to draw attention to the implied message the organisation conveys about the status and importance of the group. In our experience these problems, especially early on, often arise at an administrative level and a friendly but clear conversation with the person responsible for room bookings is often enough. However, the difficulties can be more serious – see Chapter 9.

TASK MAINTENANCE

A different kind of boundary is around what the task of the group is. As discussed in Chapter 3, there are several ways in which a staff support group can go 'off task'. A helpful 'star' for the facilitator to steer by is the statement by Bolton and Roberts (1994: 164) that 'support is needed to enable staff to face rather than evade difficult issues'. At times it may be obvious that difficulties are being evaded – long silence or talk about matters unrelated to work like holiday plans or a film someone saw last night. Here the facilitator has a limited number of options: to wait and see what happens; to comment on the avoidance of anything to do with work; or if there does seem to be a connection, to comment on the possible link if this would be accepted by the group – e.g. the relevance of the film plot to a situation at work. The intervention may or may not be effective, but the facilitator is at least clear in his or her own mind that the group is avoiding difficulties and needs to be helped back on task, possibly with the offer of a hypothesis, if the facilitator has one, about why this might be happening.

There will be other times when the group is squarely on target. There has been an untoward incident, or a staff member has been severely shaken by an event, and this is openly and sensitively talked about in the group. Here the facilitator's role may be to do very little, to let the mutual support available in the group do the work. The facilitator's main responsibility will be to check out before the group ends the level of distress in those who have spoken and also in those who have not and who may be holding back their own feelings. It is important that staff can leave the room and go back into their functioning work roles, so the facilitator may need to intervene some time before the end of the session to bring the group back to a more calm and contained state, if necessary suggesting what members could do after the session if they need further support.

Often a group is somewhere between these two: touching on recent or current events but keeping it relatively safe, avoiding the more painful or uncomfortable aspects or potential discord between those present in the group. An anxiety arousing risky event may be discussed in humorous terms – perhaps an example of the 'gallows humour' well-known among staff who work on a daily basis with life-threatening situations. Frustration or anger over an organisational failure may be blamed entirely on senior managers who are not in the room, with no thought about their own responsibilities or the complexities of the situation. Uncertainty about the best way to handle a tricky situation may be responded to with a demand for written rules or guidelines rather than acknowledging the anxiety about getting something wrong. The question for the facilitator here is whether to let the conversation continue on its present level or try to take it closer to what may be the heart of the matter – what Rifkind (1995) has called the 'tension point'. The concept of 'defences' is helpful here. 'Everyone needs and uses defences at some time – the question is, to what extent and when?' (Brown and Pedder 1979: 25). The group may be defending themselves against emotional pain or conflict, using humour, intellectualisation, projection of blame, or just plain denial – 'no, everything is fine thank you'. If this is what the facilitator feels is happening the delicate task is to look for an intervention that will invite the group to go a little closer to the 'tension point', but in a way that doesn't push too hard and doesn't sound like the facilitator is trying to read people's minds. This leads us on to looking at types of intervention.

TYPES OF INTERVENTION

As we noted in Chapter 3 there are some types of intervention to be avoided: those that suggest a detached 'sitting in judgement' attitude on the part of the facilitator, that seek to interpret an individual's hidden or unconscious motives, that increase anxiety or regression in the group, or that encourage exploration of personal fantasies that group members may have about the facilitator. In other words many of the interventions that would be central in an analytic group are not appropriate because they take the group to places it is not designed for, and risk undermining the sense of safety in the group.

This still leaves a number if interventions in the group therapist's tool bag to make use of, as well as others that may be more familiar in the settings of a seminar, supervision or discussion group. The flexibility of the staff support group means that the facilitator needs to be prepared to move between different types of intervention. These are some that are likely to be of use.

Open questions

These are questions where the facilitator doesn't have a particular aim other than to help the group get started, to interact, or reconnect with itself. The facilitator may, for example, ask if anyone has anything they want to talk about, ask how others are feeling about a subject being discussed by two or three people, or ask about an issue that had been discussed in a previous group.

Encouraging empathy

When a member takes a risk and shares something that exposes some vulnerability it is important, both for them and for the group, that they get a supportive, empathic response and are not left feeling ignored or rejected. This may happen naturally, but if it doesn't the facilitator can help by saying something like, 'that must have been very difficult for you', or, 'I wonder if others have felt like that too'.

Asking for clarification or information

Sometimes it is useful simply to ask someone who is expressing frustration or dissatisfaction about a situation to be more specific, so that the discussion is based on what actually happened rather than on assumptions or stereotypes. For example, a complaint about the insensitivity of a manager or about lack of resources (both quite common complaints) can easily lead to an animated but unproductive rehash of past grievances. It is more useful for the facilitator to get the group to examine the particular incident that gave rise to the complaint, as the reality is usually more complex and nuanced than people's immediate reactions. The facilitator can make good use of their ignorance by asking questions like, 'What normally happens in a situation like this?' or 'What would the alternatives have been?' Such questions demonstrate both a willingness to learn and also open up the discussion and reveal potential differing points of view within the team.

Modelling

Whether intended or not, everything the facilitator does in a group offers a model of how to behave that the members may emulate. A show of interest, a thoughtful question, an expression of concern or an admission of doubt, these are all behaviours that members may borrow, knowingly or not, in their own interactions. Perhaps most useful of all is when the facilitator models a reflective, thoughtful attitude that tries to understand rather than pass judgement.

Self-disclosure

An important question for a group facilitator is whether, and how much, to say about their own experience. This is a potentially helpful intervention but also one with risks attached. It is one of the ways the facilitator can demonstrate an equality in their relationship with the group, letting the group see them as a real person rather than as distant and uninvolved.

Example

The members of a staff support group in a children's hospice were talking about the recent admission of a number of very small babies that could die at any time, and what they could say to the parents who did not know how long their child would live. The facilitator felt tears pricking his eyes as he listened, and acknowledged to the group that he felt moved by the discussion.

It can also be a helpful way to normalise guilty or shameful experiences – for example if the facilitator admits to a past error of judgement or moment of great anxiety. However, such self-disclosure can backfire if it focuses attention on the facilitator rather than the group.

Example

The staff group on a residential unit for severely handicapped children was discussing the problem of older siblings visiting with their parents and then walking off with some of the unit's toys. The facilitator wanted to moderate what seemed to him to be a rather moralistic attitude towards adolescents, and shared with the group his own experience of having shoplifted as a teenager. This was met with curiosity about the facilitator's delinquent tendencies rather than the hoped for sharing of similar adolescent exploits by the staff.

A good general guide is that the facilitator is aware of the aim in making a disclosure, and that it is made in response to the needs of the group rather than the needs or wishes of the facilitator. Humphreys in Chapter 13 (pp. 162–72) illustrates the appropriate and timely use of self-disclosure.

Challenge or confrontation

This is something that should be done very rarely, and normally only to the group as a whole rather than one individual. One of the functions of the facilitator is to ensure that no one feels isolated and unsupported in the group, and that any confrontation in the group is balanced by support. There may be occasions when the group is avoiding an issue and the facilitator has exhausted all other means to overcome this. The group's response to a direct challenge is likely to depend on the degree of trust the facilitator has built up and is not to be recommended early in the group's life.

Commenting on parallel group process

Parallel process refers to a close similarity between something happening in the group and events outside it even when on the surface they seem unrelated.

> *Example*
> A member of a nurses' support group told the group how it could affect the whole shift when one member of the team had a negative attitude. The facilitator recognized this as something that happened in the group as well, but had not been spoken openly about. He used the opportunity of the nurse's comment to ask if the same thing sometimes happened in the group and what the group might be able to do about it.

This is as near as the staff support group facilitator should probably get to making an interpretation, and it can be helpful when approached in a tentative way and focused on the team as a whole.

Teams that work with emotionally needy clients can find themselves buffeted by a range of painful emotions as they strive, and inevitably sometimes fail, to provide what clients are consciously or unconsciously asking for. In Chapter 13 Humphreys describes a common reaction to feeling inadequate in the face of demands for more or better care, which is for the team to mirror or repeat this feeling in relation to the people they feel should be caring for *them* – the senior staff or managers. Although not ignoring reality components like staff shortages, the facilitator can help the team to see that they may be experiencing similar feelings of rejection or helplessness that their patients or clients are experiencing. If the facilitator can do this, it can help the team understand and manage their own reactions that otherwise may simply feel strangely punitive or rejecting towards the patients.

The group as a seminar

There may be occasions when the group briefly becomes a supervision group or seminar and the facilitator's role changes to a more educative one.

For example, staff unsure how to respond to someone who has just been bereaved may find it helpful to know the stages of normal bereavement if this is outside the team's knowledge; the discussion of some problem behaviour the team had not encountered before might be followed by some useful diagnostic information; a team struggling with an issue they want to discuss with senior managers may find it useful to consider management structures and how to approach them. The facilitator should not assume they are the sole source of helpful information as there may be much knowledge or wisdom in the group. This switch from spontaneous unstructured discussion to something more structured should be viewed in terms of whether this empowers the group to face rather than evade a difficulty, and whether the group moves back into its unstructured format afterwards.

WORKING WITH FEELINGS

Where membership changes from session to session, as is usually the case in groups for staff who work shifts, each session of a staff support group has to be treated more or less as a one-off. Lacking the continuity of membership of a therapeutic or a sensitivity group, those attending are not emotionally 'held' by the developing relationship of trust between members. Staff may feel more or less safe according to which of their colleagues are present in a particular session. This will lead some staff to be cautious about expressing their feelings, and to feel very uneasy if someone shows their feelings too strongly. It is not uncommon that if someone becomes visibly upset and tearful in a group, this somehow percolates through the whole team and attendance at the following session plummets. As Lederberg stated (1998: 276), 'In staff support groups the members work together all day and extreme emotion is not containable'.

It is important for the facilitator to keep watch on the level of emotion in the group – how much there is, how close it is to the surface, how comfortable people are with it. The facilitator does this partly by keeping an eye on everyone, including the silent members – not staring intently, just glancing round every so often – and partly by noticing their own state of feeling as a kind of barometer in the group.

Example

A normally cheerful and robust member of a group for the staff of a large community mental health team broke down in tears when describing the shock for one of her patients whose young son had been involved in a near fatal accident on a school river trip. It turned out that her own brother had drowned when she was 16, and the pain of that time had come flooding back, taking her and the rest of the group by surprise. Outwardly the group was very supportive, but quickly changed the subject.

> The facilitator sensed that the impact on the group had gone underground and that the other members were anxious not to say anything that might upset her further. About ten minutes before the end he gently suggested that this is what had happened. This provided an opportunity for the person concerned to say that she felt okay now and that it had helped her to be able to cry in the group. Nevertheless only four people came to the next session and it was two or three weeks before attendance was back to full strength.

In this case the equilibrium of a normally well-functioning team member had been temporarily shaken by an event with powerful personal echoes for her. The group in its turn took a little while to recover its equilibrium. By intervening as he did the facilitator helped to bring the group back to the anxiety that was being avoided. As often happens, the individual who had expressed her emotion felt better, but those who had avoided theirs took longer to recover. One wonders if the group would have recovered quicker if the facilitator had not gone along with the change of subject.

SURVIVING

The presence of a staff support group in an organisation has to some extent a meaning and an impact beyond what actually goes on in the group. Staff support groups can be both idealised and denigrated, seen as a beacon of hope or a threat to the smooth running of the organisation. They can be the subject of myths and opinions among those who never attend or who work in different parts of the organisation. Even among those who attend there may be a gap between the idea of the group and its reality. A new doctor on a psychiatric unit told the facilitator that one of the reasons he had applied for the job was because the unit had a staff support group, yet in the group he rarely talked about any personal issues and acted as if his only role was to support the nursing staff in the group.

In the face of these opposing currents of feeling surrounding the group, one of the basic tasks of the facilitator is to survive – to stay the course – and to ensure that the group survives, at least until such time as its ending may be formally agreed (see Chapter 7). This may mean turning up and staying in the room waiting for someone to arrive, discussing with those staff who do come how they can encourage their colleagues to attend, reviewing reasons for sudden cancellations with the manager who commissioned the group, and generally conveying the message that you intend to do the job you were asked to do and that obstacles to this will be discussed and sympathetically worked with. Of course this can be very hard in practice, as McGowan vividly describes in Chapter 9. What is important in the facilitator's role is what he or she represents and demonstrates by adopting this approach: not retaliating, not giving up, not being destroyed or taking their ball home; surviving by seeking to understand the processes going on (if possible with the help of their own supervisor or mentor), by discussing them with those involved, by responding to the group's questions about how they cope. This is not about being superhuman or unaffected by stressful events, more about retaining and demonstrating the belief that we are all human, that actions can be understood, and that sharing experiences and perceptions is often a good place to start.

In the next chapter we look in more detail at the questions and problems that commonly arise as the group develops and how the facilitator can address these.

Chapter 6

Some common problems and ways of responding to them

Phil Hartley and David Kennard

Once it has been agreed to establish a staff support group, its members and the facilitator are usually curious, and often anxious about how it will be. This chapter will discuss some common problems that arise and suggest ways of responding to them. In our experience, and those of other facilitators, there are difficulties common to most staff support groups, if not all. The aim of the response to any problem is to make the group a safe enough place in which its members can talk to one another. It is not, as in a therapy group, for the members to explore the origins of the problem and how they relate to it, though this may occur as a by-product in a safe enough group. Common anticipatory concerns have been discussed in the previous chapter, but as the group unfolds a range of questions and concerns will surface for the facilitator to respond to.

- Will poor attendance close the group?
- Will there be long silences?
- What happens if people get upset?
- What will we talk about?
- Do we have to attend?
- Will managers be coming?
- Can we leave the room to deal with a crisis?
- Will I be analysed?
- Will there be a review of the group?

A NOTE ON THE WIDER IMPACT OF STAFF SUPPORT GROUPS

How these questions and problems are dealt with can have ramifications beyond the group itself. The staff support group is a living learning experience for its members, in which they experience how common group situations are dealt with in a variety of settings, e.g. educational, clinical, team, organisational. Common problems like conflict, distress, silence and poor punctuality, are not confined to a staff support group and occur in many situations where people meet and try to work together. In a study of the effectiveness of staff support groups Thomas argues that they 'offer more than just peer support and time to reflect, they also help nurses to develop interpersonal skills within a safe environment' (Thomas 1995: 37). Staff support groups, more than other professional meetings, have powerful impacts on their members that go well beyond the group's boundaries, and the ways the members experience problems between them being managed will have a particular resonance, for good or bad. Well managed common problems in staff support groups provide an *in vivo* training in managing similar situations in other settings.

WILL POOR ATTENDANCE CLOSE THE GROUP?

Group members will always have conflicting demands on their time that can make punctual and reliable attendance problematic. The start and finish time can be seen as a group boundary, and the most usual forms of 'boundary testing' are poor punctuality and attendance. Most readers will recognize and have thoughts about why one person is perpetually late for meetings. Few will think it is just because they are a poor time-keeper. The way in which they enter meetings influences the private speculations about why someone is late. Meetings in which many members are late, or that do not start on time because people are chatting, may suggest an avoidance of the issue to be discussed, or an organisational culture. Readers may privately think, or discuss with colleagues, that someone is late because they 'like to make an entrance' or 'give an impression of being very busy', or have issues with authority. It would be relatively unusual for this to be discussed with the person. If it is an organisational culture, discussing it is probably actively avoided and new members are faced with a dilemma of whether to be punctual or not. The difference in a staff support group is that it is something that should be discussed.

The facilitator has already negotiated the start and finish time and explained the importance of punctuality in helping the group feel reliable and safe. Whatever the legitimacy of lateness, it is still a communication that something else is more important than the group. To gently enquire why someone is late can facilitate a conversation about its impact on the group members, or allow the latecomer to express dissatisfaction or ambivalence with the group. It is important to actively and seriously consider whether persistent problems with punctuality are because the timing of the group is difficult. This is not likely to be the case if it was properly discussed when the group was set up, but something may have been overlooked. The facilitator should always be mindful and attentive to the organisational life outside the group. Actively considering causes of lateness, or leaving early demonstrates this. This connects the group to the organisation and what issues influence the membership. In our experience, providing the timing of the group has been adequately attended to, changing the time of the group rarely, almost never, improves attendance. Milton and Davison (1997: 143) note 'action often occurred in place of thinking'. Therefore, changing time (action) means that thinking does not occur about what the behaviour (lateness) means. The facilitator's role is to help the group members think and talk to one another, by drawing attention to the issue and not avoiding it. Milton and Davidson (1997: 143) go on '. . . in fact it seemed that rather than being a space for thinking the group was used as a repository for unbearable states of mind'. To ignore what poor punctuality is communicating is to deposit something unbearable into the group. The longer the issue is avoided, the more unbearable it becomes to talk about, though the facilitator should not leap on any minor infraction as a crucial communication, more keep in mind it needs attending to. Lateness may indicate an avoidance of painful emotions between group members, or with their work. Requests to change times or shorten the group taken at face value, do not help the members work on these issues with one another, or to support each other.

Example

A new manager of a service does not attend an established staff support group, in which punctuality has usually been good. Following a meeting between the facilitator and the new manager to discuss the group, the manager decides to attend. She openly questions the value of the group but admits to not having been to one before. In subsequent sessions group members increasingly give their apologies for lateness or having to leave early because of unavoidable commitments. The new manager suggests reviewing the timing and frequency of the group. The suggestion is met with apathy and impotence. The facilitator suggests that it would be helpful to think about the manager's suggestion. Previous attempts to facilitate thinking about the reasons for apologies have been fruitless. Consideration is given to moving the time of the group, but it is felt that it is already at the most convenient time.

The manager's suggestion gives the facilitator a legitimate opportunity to ask if members' commitments other than the group were real, or connected with what was happening in the group. At first there were blank looks and denials, but prompted to wonder when they started to arrive late or leave early, they connected it with the manager's attendance. The facilitator asking why, helped people to talk about worrying their manager did not want the group, and that they should do other things. The manager reassured them that although sceptical, she genuinely wanted to see what it was like. This meant people could discuss the importance of attending punctually and regularly to give her an accurate impression of what the group was like and discuss their anxieties she may want the group to stop.

The manager, by suggesting changing the time of the group, was taking management 'action' to a perceived problem. It was also an attack on the group because it colluded with reasons for not attending, rather than reinforcing the boundary. By taking the manager's suggestion seriously competing demands were actively considered, so validating the manager's role, while giving the group thinking time. The unbearable state of mind was anxiety about what the manager thought of the group and her power to stop it. Whereas for the manager it was feeling unfamiliar and exposed in a new situation.

Boundary testing: attendance

Poor attendance, or a drop in the number of staff attending a group, is difficult for all concerned. The facilitator can feel anxious, and despondent that their time is being wasted. The remaining group members are under more pressure to fill the time and have to think of things to say. They may feel guilty for being there, if their colleagues have other urgent commitments that mean they cannot attend. In our experience, it is a natural part of a group cycle when the numbers drop. However, without attention being paid to it, low numbers make a group problematic or untenable. Poor attendance in the early stages of a group is particularly difficult. There is a dread of sitting looking at one another, and not knowing what to say. Tense silence follows a period of anxious conversation, often ultimately leading to resigned and apathetic periods of silence. The way the facilitator manages his or her feelings at this stage is crucial to the group's survival. Too much anxiety or irritation is experienced by group members as punitive and is likely to exacerbate the problem. Letting the silence continue is experienced as being 'too much like therapy' and causes resentment.

As with punctuality, the timing of the group has been negotiated to facilitate attendance. It is not unreasonable to expect people to turn up. However, in the early stages they are likely to prioritise their activity outside the group, more than their work in the group. It is likely there are good reasons why people have not attended. It is usual for the first one or two sessions to have reasonable numbers attending, but they often drop after that. Whether senior staff attend is a significant culture carrier at this stage, and sets an example to junior staff. There is often a request to re-negotiate the timing of the group. It is tempting to do this, but should be resisted because of the reasons stated earlier in this chapter. However, it should not be dismissed out of hand either. It is helpful to discuss how the group members have found the sessions to date, and to ask them to speculate how other people are finding the group. It is important to have agreed guidelines (Lederberg 1998) about discussing absent members first. They should not be spoken about in person, rather the group members are summarising how the group is experienced by the team. The facilitator can wonder whether people's experience of the group is influencing attendance and what may help if it is.

Example

Having met with a team for well attended sessions to discuss a staff support group, and agreed senior staff would attend, after three sessions of the group starting just three people turn up. One of the senior staff, who also commissioned the group, gives his apologies because of a pressing alternative engagement. There is no doubt that this engagement is genuine, but it reoccurs several times. The number of people attending each session falls to two or three people. The sessions continue, but are difficult and stilted with the people attending feeling they have to fill the time. The facilitator asks in each session why people think the numbers are low and what practical steps can be made to address it. Helpful suggestions are made to remind staff, like putting up notices and entries in the staff diary. The facilitator encourages the staff to advertise the group by word of mouth, asking colleagues to attend and to discuss their experience of being in a group with low numbers. This helps non-attendees to realise that deciding not to attend has a consequence for their colleagues.

The facilitator thought about whether to discuss the manager's non-attendance with him in private or in the group. She decided to say something next time the manager attended so that the other group members would see the manager being asked to attend because he was an important member and to set an example – in particular because of his position and because he had commissioned the group. Although a difficult conversation it was important that the group members saw the boundary being reinforced.

In this example attendance was a constant issue and needed constant attention, though attendance picked up in general and the manager came much more regularly. Word of mouth is by far the best way to get regular attendees, and it is helpful for those who do attend to feel they can encourage their peers to do the same. However, this type of group is 'not for all' and that should be respected. As we have made it clear that attendance is better optional than compulsory it would be better to close this section with a reminder that although good attendance is important, it should be recognized that staff support groups are not the only form of staff support and some staff may find other forums meet their needs.

WILL THERE BE LONG SILENCES?

It is common for there to be silences at the beginning of a session. Prompting group members to start is usually helpful. Asking 'How have things been?' or 'What would you like to talk about?' helps to break the ice. Sometimes group members request to take turns or have a rota of who should start the session. If there is a strong feeling it would help, it can be a useful structure, but silences will still often occur. Why is this? Silences have different meanings and qualities. The facilitator who is not too anxious will be able to 'tune in' and speculate about it. The silence may be tense or relaxed, contemplative or apathetic. Whatever the quality, it is not helpful to let it go on for more than two or three minutes. Long silences produce discomfort and people wonder who will be first to break it, or think they will not be the first to do so. The silence assumes a life of its own and at its worst is highly uncomfortable and affects future attendance. The facilitator can comment, 'It seems difficult to start today', which is usually enough to get things going. If that does not work, asking people how they feel about the silence helps the participants to discuss what is happening. If that does not work either, the facilitator may try gently asking, 'Is it me, or do other people find this silence tense, or difficult which makes it hard to start?' The aim is to draw people's attention to what is happening between them, and to help them talk about it and wonder why.

We have sat in groups where the silence has lasted for a long time, up to half the session for example. This is highly unusual, and more likely to occur in a well-established group. Sometimes a silence is not negative and people are enjoying doing nothing and being in one another's company, though if someone states this we are sceptical and more likely to think they are rationalising their anxiety. It may be true, but it is useful to remind people that it is their time to discuss the task or theme they wanted the group for.

Example

A member of a staff support group gets upset and tearful. Initially people are supportive and talk to her. As she gains her composure people struggle to say much and become silent. Fairly quickly the facilitator asks what people are thinking. This prompts them to talk, and the facilitator asks why it was difficult for them to say much after the distressed group member stopped crying. People discuss feeling they don't know what to say, or do not want to make things worse. These are common and normal reactions and important for the distressed group member to hear. She responds (as is often the case) that she feels better for crying and people do not have to say anything.

The following week many of the same people are there, including the member who was upset. People are reluctant to start and the prompts previously mentioned are ineffective. The silence felt uncomfortable and people seemed in their own worlds, sitting still with little eye contact. The facilitator is thinking about how the distressed person had been through the week, and felt slightly irritated that nothing had been said. He decided to ask the person, how she felt. She said she had felt much better and had been fine. No one joined with her and the silence continued. The facilitator privately hypothesised she had not been all right and that the silence was connected. As he had made several attempts to encourage people to say more he asked someone looking less introverted than the rest, what they made of the silence. He then asked other people to speculate. It transpired the distressed person had been upset after the group and had taken time out causing some considerable inconvenience. People were worried about upsetting her again, but also irritated that she had taken time out. People said they were unsure how she was and did not want to upset her and risk the inconvenience again. This allowed a conversation about how they try and support one another when they are affected by their work, without causing too much disruption.

WHAT HAPPENS IF PEOPLE GET UPSET?

People do not generally come to work to display strong emotions to their colleagues, or to have to help others deal with them, unless this is part of their role. It is often considered unprofessional to have emotional displays at work. Despite this, it is not unusual and people do feel things very strongly, regardless of whether or not the feelings are openly expressed. Menzies (1959) described how nursing staff distance themselves from the emotional impact of their work by concentrating on work procedures or structures. The staff support group challenges this by its very existence, by saying staff are affected by their work. Despite this, it is often quite difficult for staff to discuss their feelings about their work, and if they do display emotion it can be difficult for colleagues to witness and bear it. There is also a danger that one or two individuals in the group are seen as the ones who are distressed, or angry. By keeping the feelings located in the individual and denying their universality, the group members maintain the problem in the other person, creating significant difficulties for the individual and the facilitator. The facilitator has a dilemma. Lederberg (1998: 295) warns that 'the facilitator must help the group acknowledge the universality of human emotions', but also 'shield a member from overexposure'. The group dynamics inhibit universality and combined with an individual's schemas (Bamber 2006), can make over exposure more likely. Lederberg predicts that if members feel they have disclosed too much this can lead to the group 'self destructing' but returning (as in the last clinical example) to 'safer levels of discourse' is protective. Individuals may from time to time relate to more personal material depending on their circumstances, for example bereavement or divorce, or remembering their own experiences because of parallels at work. The staff support group would be lacking in empathy to deny time to acknowledge this type of distress, but to focus on it too much would be to deviate from the agreed aim of the group and risk it having a different function. The facilitator's role is to help group members not to over-disclose, and to help the group maintain its 'safe discourse' by concentrating on its aims while accepting when other circumstances demand necessary attention.

Example: distress

A staff member working with a client who has been sexually abused, has been very affected by the client self-injuring. In the group she says she feels responsible for the client's injury and upset by her history. She tearfully says it reminds her of some of her own issues. There is an increasing anxiety in the group at what she may disclose. The group members had agreed not to use the group to discuss their own histories. People look uneasily at one another and shift uncomfortably, because they know she is likely to say she has been sexually abused, or has self-injured.

The facilitator intervenes, reminding the person that although she and others are, of course, reminded of their own experiences at work, that they are here to discuss work-related issues, not their own. The facilitator then asks a couple of questions about how the client self-injured and why the staff member felt responsible, so bringing the focus back to the work task, not the individual's history. The facilitator asks if other people have felt responsible when someone has self-injured so protecting the member from over disclosing and her feelings are normalised by the experience being identified with by other staff.

Example: conflict

Situations at work that cause anxiety are often ones that generate disagreement about how they should be managed. It is unusual for there to be major conflict in staff support groups, but it can occur.

The self-injuring client previously mentioned has a good relationship with her key nurse. The nurse feels her client is misunderstood and judged too harshly by her colleagues. In the group, two members accuse the key nurse of treating the client as her favourite and of not sticking to the management plan. An argument follows that becomes volatile quite quickly as allegations and counter-allegations are made. The other group members either sit in uncomfortable silence, or lapse into impotence having tried to intervene. People anxiously look at the facilitator to do something.

What the facilitator does in a situation like this will vary according to their experience of and knowledge about self-injurious behaviour. The situation described is not uncommon in teams who work with this issue. Informing the group of this can help them think about why teams respond to self-injury in this way, and puts enough distance from the immediate situation to discuss it more calmly. People will often look for a solution to conflict and the group may move into discussing clinical management plans. This is usually the function of a different meeting and not an appropriate use of a staff support group.

An open conflict is often related not just to the incident being discussed, but can have been brewing for some time. It is helpful to ask the other group members how they feel having witnessed the angry exchange. Some group members will want to focus on the solution or take one side or the other, but the facilitator is trying to get people to say how they are affected by the argument. This serves two purposes – it limits the probability of further argument as the protagonists realise the impact they have had on their colleagues: and group members begin to realise that the impact is not just on the members of the staff support group, but that the disagreement affects their working relationships in the team. Having cleared the air it is helpful to suggest using one of the team's usual clinical meetings to discuss the management plan for this client.

The key nurse is likely to feel very anxious about the allegations. Asking how she is affected by her client's self-injury, and asking other people the same question, focuses on their universal experience. In this scenario it was impotence and failure, with some (the key nurse) trying harder to compensate and others distancing themselves and giving up to avoid their feelings. Once the feelings and their impact have been expressed, care planning can be easier. This can be discussed in other appropriate meetings, as can the underlying reasons for the key nurse possibly treating the client as her favourite. The staff support group can usefully highlight a team dynamic and reasons for it, but its primary aim is not to resolve them.

WHAT WILL WE TALK ABOUT?

How the group will be used is part of the contracting arrangements and is discussed in Chapter 4 in relation to the aims of the group. Agreeing on an aim or task of the group does not take away the anxiety about what will be discussed. As previously stated in this chapter reminding people of the group's task helps to deal with deviations and silence. The anxiety behind this question masks a deeper question: how will we talk to one another about our work?

The previous section stressed the importance of universality. This is only achieved if the group members can share their experiences. The problem for the facilitator is how to make people feel safe enough to talk. Asking why it is difficult tends to produce relevant but automatic answers. For example, 'we are trained not to show our feelings' or 'we are professionals and try to be objective'. Although this is true, common experience of the workplace and work-related stress suggests that subjective reactions are normal. Anxiety about talking to one another may cause resistance or avoidance in achieving the group's aim. The facilitator has to hypothesise to him or herself why sticking to the aim of the group is difficult. If it is in the early stages of the group, or after a difficult event (as in the above examples) the solutions to reducing anxiety and helping people to talk are described in the previous chapter. The solution to avoidance of the task depends on the nature of the hypothesis that explains the deviation from the group's aim. Even established groups that function well avoid using the time they are set up for. People say they have nothing to talk about this week, or nothing has happened, or there is silence. In our experience, when this occurs it may be because something has happened that they do not want to talk about with one another, or because the members are anxious about potential conflict in the group. Sometimes the resistance manifests itself by people talking about anything but why they agreed to set the group up.

This is a more difficult problem for the facilitator than it may seem. If the interventions already described are ineffective, the facilitator may be tempted to try too hard, to the irritation of the group members, or to lapse into defeated silence and collude with them. The way the facilitator copes with their own feelings is part of the solution. Lederberg (1998: 299) discussing over-disclosure by group members, says that staff support groups are 'definitely not a good setting in which to put trainees learning psychotherapy skills'. Coping with a group avoiding talking about something that has happened and hypothesising what it may be, is difficult, as is knowing how to respond having reached a hypothesis. Interpreting the avoidance is unhelpful as it is too easily felt as criticism. Our response to this situation is for the facilitator to say he or she feels puzzled, bemused, or 'not quite able to put my finger on it'.

When feeling like this it is important to wait and see whether one of the group members asks 'What shall we talk about?' or 'Why are we talking about this?' If this does not happen after 10 or 15 minutes (having tried interventions suggested earlier) the response depends on the maturity of the group. A mature group is one whose members tend to do much of the facilitation themselves, by asking one another questions, or who easily identify with one another. In a new or less well-functioning group, the facilitator can ask why people are not talking about what they wanted the group to be used for. It reminds them of the aim, but invites them to also analyse what is happening. The question should be asked non-critically. A puzzled enquiry engages people with the facilitator's thinking.

In a more mature and well-functioning group, particularly if they usually stick to task, asking whether the deviation suggests something is being avoided, makes them think carefully. It is usually something to ask when the facilitator has a hypothesis about what is being avoided. The question can be asked if the facilitator does not have a hypothesis, but only in groups able to tolerate the significant anxiety it will cause. Asking what is being avoided would not be a helpful intervention if there is a poor relationship between the group members and the facilitator. It is not a helpful thing to say if the facilitator is angry or anxious, or wants to do something powerful.

A useful and simple intervention that can help to rescue an otherwise sticky or becalmed meeting, and is also useful in slowing down a very animated session, is to ask about ten minutes before the end, how people have found the session today. It provides a step back from whatever has been happening in the group, and is near enough to the end for members to make quite personal comments without the risk of being asked to develop them.

Example

Staff members come to a support group on time, they talk to one another about their social lives. There is little eye contact with the facilitator. The usual fading away of conversation, as people shift into the work mode of the group does not happen. The facilitator interrupts saying it is time to start, and asking what would people like to talk about. There is silence for a few seconds before whispering between pairs of people increases to a general conversation between group members about their holidays. It is August and the staff absences and holidays have been a major disruption in the group and the team. The facilitator asks how has the week been. People pause and look at one another, there is a rising sense of anxiety. The group lapses into silence. The facilitator comments that it seems difficult to start today. The group members do not respond. After waiting for one or two minutes the facilitator asks why it is difficult for people to use the group today. It transpires that there has been an incident which, but for good luck, could have been much more serious. The team leader has been away on holiday and will have to conduct an internal enquiry on their return. Now that the incident has been mentioned in the group, the facilitator can encourage people to discuss what happened and how they are feeling about it.

DO WE HAVE TO ATTEND?

This question should be answered in the contracting stage, and is discussed in Chapter 4. It is helpful to have a set of ground rules that address predicted problems. An example of ground rules negotiated with a team are:

- to start and end sessions punctually;
- attendance is encouraged, but is on a voluntary basis;
- to send your apologies if you cannot attend;
- the group is confidential, unless there are concerns about issues of professional misconduct or unmanaged risk to self or others, in which case, confidentiality would be breached, usually after discussion in the group first;
- no material should be discussed outside the group without informing the group first;
- a respect for and willingness to listen to others. Not to unduly pressurise people into disclosing material.

There will always be occasional circumstances where ground rules are difficult to maintain. For example, people may be late, or forget to send their apologies. Well-negotiated ground rules are more of an agreement between the group members themselves, than between the group members and the facilitator. For example members sending their apologies indicates that they are holding the group in mind and treating their colleagues with respect. Negotiating ground rules is helpfully achieved by asking the group members to discuss what is needed to make the group safe enough. The facilitator's role is to help them think about the pros and cons of their discussion. It is helpful for them to be revisited, when the staff support group is reviewed.

Poor attendance has been addressed earlier in this chapter. The ground rules clearly set out that attendance is encouraged and voluntary. People do not 'have to attend', is the best way of answering the question. People usually do not want to attend when there is something about the group they do not like. It is important to try and ascertain what this is and for the other group members to discuss it.

Example
After a session in which someone was upset, and attendance was low the following week, a senior doctor asks, 'Do we have to attend this group, because I have more important things I could do each week?'

The question is often posed after a difficult experience in the group and is driven by anxiety. In this example the doctor was concerned about a senior group member being upset. Discussion revealed an important question about the value of such displays of emotion. The doctor was particularly worried about senior staff showing their feelings and how it impacted on junior staff. Management and supervision structures often encourage suppression of feelings. Junior staff learn that more senior staff are less affected by their work and that they should adopt the same attitude. When this attitude is translated into social defences, as described by Menzies (1959), feelings invoked by the work are ignored.

The staff support group that can discuss the differences in roles and responsibilities of its membership as well as the commonality of their experience is more likely to appreciate their differences with one another and less likely to attack them, for example when junior and senior staff each denigrate the other.

In the above example, the doctor questioned whether getting upset would have a negative affect on the team. What he meant was, would the team feel less able to rely on him if he got upset? It is a crucial question. In a system that expects senior staff to be omnipotent it may not be helpful for them to be perceived as not coping. The next example demonstrates that this is not always the case.

Example
A senior doctor cries in a group because of a traumatic incident. The staff support group consist of quite powerful subgroups and many people struggle to disclose their feelings. Despite this there has been a deepening respect for one another's roles, and how they are affected by their work. The team discussed how they felt about her crying and reassured the doctor they would not be adversely affected. The doctor felt sufficiently reassured, and did not have to rely on being omnipotent.

WILL THE MANAGERS BE COMING?

Staff seniority is the obvious hierarchy in the group, with arguably the facilitator the most powerful. There are other power structures – vocal influential individuals, or pairs, or blocks of staff who although junior may have a major influence on the team's culture, attitude and practice.

It can help if a group includes those from different levels in the hierarchy. Their roles 'flatten out' in the group and are reassumed when the session finishes. Hierarchal roles and power struggles are normal in teams and services, and are not left out of the staff support group. Conflict, diffidence or passivity are common responses to power issues in the staff support group. Bolton and Roberts (1994: 164) reviewing staff support and sensitivity groups stress that a 'common mistake is to use such groups to do away with differences among participants, whether differences of role, authority, or point of view'. By 'flattening out' their roles we do not argue for ignoring difference, rather that difference is not used to ignore the universality of human experience. Different disciplines often have little idea about the reality of each other's work and its frustrations. Despite having different roles, their frustrations are similar – impotence, anxiety and anger. They grow to know one another by visualising their human experience, and not only by the identity of their stereotyped role, e.g. doctor, nurse, etc. In our experience this can be particularly helpful to managers whose work is more understood and appreciated by junior staff. They in turn can see managers as less distant and omnipotent. All members of the hierarchy despite their different roles can come to understand they often struggle with similar feelings. This common experience develops mutual understanding.

In the last example, the doctor crying was seen and treated as a person who was upset which in that moment was little to do with her professional identity. People responded empathically and showed their own feelings to her. The doctor's role remained intact because in the group the members had come to know one another as people and less as rivalrous and antagonistic subgroups or different disciplines.

When line managers and their staff are in the same group, staff often worry about being judged negatively by their manager. Managers, like the doctor in the last example, worry about being seen as weak. Despite these complex issues, we think the aim continues to be the universality of the human experience. In practice, the success of this depends on the ability of the group and facilitator to discuss and manage their differences and similarities with one another and not to use that knowledge destructively, either in or out of the group. To ensure that Bolton and Roberts' (1994) concerns that differences between group members are not avoided and ours that the universality of human experience is attended to means discussing how group members' feelings are influenced by their different responsibilities is crucial.

CAN WE LEAVE THE ROOM TO DEAL WITH A CRISIS?

Bearing in mind 'boundary challenges from outside the group' in Chapter 5 the easy answer to this question is, yes, providing the crisis is not one of a succession of boundary challenges, or a crisis that is not really a crisis. Preventing people from leaving is too anxiety provoking and distracting. It is better that people feel able to leave, sort out a situation and return to discuss its actual severity and impact. Providing the organisation is taking the staff support group seriously and providing adequate staffing cover, staff leaving is rare. The fact that the question is asked, and thought about, reflects the reality of the staff working outside the group and as previously discussed is something the facilitator should know about.

Example

A staff support group for mental health professionals takes place in a room on a corridor just off the main ward. There is a loud commotion, and distress outside the door, which is not quickly responded to by staff on the ward. The group members exchange concerned looks and glance at the facilitator. He asks whether they want to see what is happening. Two staff leave, deal with the situation and return after a few minutes.

In a well-functioning group, it can be almost as if this disturbance did not happen and it has little impact on what is being discussed. It is important though to ask a little about what actually happened. This reduces anxiety and fantasy of the remaining group members about the incident. It is also helpful to ask what people thought was happening which allows people to express their anxieties. Often this is enough and the issue can be left as a minor distraction. On occasions, it reveals much more about the staff's working lives. Simply asking 'does it happen a lot?' can open up a catalogue of previously unmentioned stressful situations.

WILL I BE ANALYSED?

This is a common question or anxiety that psychological therapists are confronted with. In the staff support group it is based on fact. The facilitator is analysing what is said and what is happening. We argue unconscious process should not be interpreted, but used to inform facilitating questions that help the group to consider what is happening between them. Adopting a genuine and friendly stance, rather than distant and closed, goes some way to managing people's perceptions. In our experience it is often the most anxious and sceptical group members that ask whether they are being analysed. We find it helpful to say that we are thinking about what is happening in the group and will usually share our thoughts. As with other scenarios asking what the other group members think involves discussion and takes the concern seriously. In reality it is often the group members who analyse each other much more than the facilitator does. Wondering with them about this, brings into the open a normal human interaction and reduces the group's need to attribute 'magical thinking' to the facilitator.

WILL THERE BE A REVIEW OF THE GROUP?

It is helpful to agree a period after which the group will be reviewed, and in a long-term group to do this on a regular basis. The review may decide to change structure, or task, a ground rule, or even close a group. Thomas (1995: 38) suggests that it takes six months to develop a cohesive support group, and that the benefits diminish slightly after the first year. Our experience suggests that the benefits are also likely to fluctuate as a consequence of how much staff turnover there is, which may vary from a stable membership to rapid turnover, or a mix of new and longer term members. In an ongoing group a review will allow members who joined after the group started to contribute to decisions about its aims and ground rules. We would suggest that a review after the first 6 months and 12 months and thereafter at yearly intervals is probably about right.

If a group is struggling or has become an aversive experience for the staff, a review can allow it to be terminated in a planned way. In other situations a review provides an opportunity to look at how well the group is meeting its aims. Where the benefits are less than hoped for, it can lead to a discussion by the group of what the obstacles are and what can be done about them. It is also an opportunity to provide the facilitator with feedback on how helpful members find his or her interventions.

Reviews can be carried out in different ways, each with their own pros and cons. Chapter 8 on evaluation will outline the pros and cons of different approaches to reviewing a staff support group.

CONCLUSION

There are many problems that can and will confront the facilitator of a staff support group. The common thread running through this chapter is that the more the group members are involved in their solution, the more likely it is to be successful. The facilitator's main intervention is to try and get the group members to think about the cause of the problem and how to manage it. It is not possible for the facilitator to provide solutions on his or her own. He or she must be prepared to at times feel uncomfortable, challenged, and impotent, while genuinely curious and interested in the group members' experience of their work.

Chapter 7

Ending a staff support group

Phil Hartley and David Kennard

There are various ways in which staff support groups can end. Some are planned or by mutual consent, some unhelpfully are unplanned or imposed.
   Endings that are planned or by mutual consent can include:

- end of the contracted number of sessions;
- decided on during a review;
- the facilitator leaving;
- notice of withdrawal of funding (sudden loss of funding may be an unplanned ending).

Endings that are unplanned or imposed can include:

- poor attendance;
- change in attitude to the staff support group by its members;
- sudden withdrawal of funding;
- burnout of the facilitator.

The experience of the group members, good or bad, significantly influences how a group ends. This chapter will describe the ways in which staff support groups close, the issues that are raised and how the facilitator may approach them.
   Like therapy groups, a support group's ending may have conscious and unconscious resonances for their members. The ending can arouse powerful emotions connected with loss, rejection, disappointment, anger and guilt. Unlike therapy groups, it is not the facilitator's role to explore the origins of these feelings and their connection with other events in the group members' lives. It is to accept them as part of their feelings about the group ending. The ending of a group may generate little reaction, or feelings of relief. Again, it is not the facilitator's role to interpret this reaction as a defence against other feelings. It is important to hold in mind that behind the members' expressed feelings there may be unexpressed or unconscious feelings. With this in mind, they can be recognized if the group members

make their own connections, rather than discussed in depth. People may be encouraged to make their own arrangements to work through them, if it is appropriate to do so.

ENDINGS THAT ARE PLANNED OR BY MUTUAL CONSENT

Planned endings for the purpose of this book are defined as those where some notice is given. The ending may be known well ahead of time, or may be only a few weeks away. A rule of thumb can be that the longer the group has been running the longer a period of notice should be. A group running for two years or more may require a three-month notice period. A group running for less than one year needs less time, perhaps a month. It is always desirable to negotiate the notice period with the group members. A notice period is needed, so that the group members can work through any feelings caused by the group ending. This may include their feelings towards, and relationship with the facilitator.

Time-limited groups are often set up to see what a staff support group is like, or to meet a specific aim with the ending negotiated from the start.

End of a contracted number of sessions

The facilitator will probably be considering what his or her experience of the group has been like. The same question needs posing to the group members. It can be rewarding, or difficult, but necessary to hear the answer. Whatever the answer, the next question can be, how will it be without the group? Sometimes it is only when faced with the loss of a staff support group, that teams come to value its usefulness and want to think how it may be replaced. In research settings some staff support group facilitators use questionnaires and/or interviews to answer how has the group been. Others, probably the majority, will ask the question directly. Using questionnaires or objective measure will be discussed in more detail in Chapter 8.

Example

A staff support group was contracted to run for 20 sessions to see whether a team wanted to use one in the longer term. This group was well attended and from the start people valued the chance to talk about their work. It was a well-established team, who wanted to develop staff support in response to a service audit. Early in the group's life, people began to acknowledge that it would be missed when the trial period came to an end. Evaluating the group was an important part of its commissioning. The evaluation was done by a discussion of whether, and how the group had helped. An important part of the general discussion was how the team would feel when the group stopped. They worked in a residential unit. The impact of their work would continue whether the group finished or not. This was influential in the team wanting a staff support group to continue as a permanent feature of their work. The general discussion asked about their experience of the facilitator, and what they would want of one in the future. The evaluation concluded that the group should continue. It was re-commissioned with the same facilitator.

Ending from a review

A review of the group can be an opportunity for the ending to be planned by the commissioning organisation, or the group members or the facilitator. A review can conclude that ending the group is desirable either because it has come to the end of its useful life, or because is not helping. Thomas (1995) suggests groups tend to have a natural life cycle beyond which members' satisfaction with them reduces. A review is a useful point to plan an ending. It is a natural punctuation in the life of the group and considering whether or when it should end part of that process. The review can also ask, should there be a different facilitator? Changing facilitators is an ending of sorts.

Example

A group that had been running for two years ended after a review concluded that a persistent problem with poor attendance was unlikely to be resolved. The low numbers meant an unviable and uneconomic group for the organisation, and poor use of the facilitator's and her employer's time. Low numbers had persisted despite various attempts to increase the membership. The review concluded that the group had been valuable for a few regular attenders, but not for the majority of people who could have attended. A one-month notice period was negotiated.

Previous reviews had analysed various reasons for poor attendance, which was explained as systemic pressures. The facilitator thought it was more to do with irresolvable differences between senior staff and what they wanted from the group. Not surprisingly, senior staff members who were uncomfortable with talking about the impact of their work attended less than those who were more comfortable doing so. Senior nurses had most problems attending because of their organisational responsibilities, while other senior staff from different disciplines did manage to attend.

The departments in the unit the group was set up for decided that there should be an alternative session which was called a 'case discussion group', which would run at the same time, but in a different format allowing different teams to rotate attendance, rather than the previously mixed membership.

The facilitator's role in this discussion was to remind the group members there was a long history of staff groups failing because members did not find them useful. The repeated failings of the staff support groups suggested a more entrenched problem than was being recognized, namely failure to manage differences between senior staff. Privately the facilitator thought renaming the group case discussion, allowed the senior nurses to feel they could safely contribute more, but was doubtful that the new group would survive. (The facilitator left the organisation and was not in a position to find out whether the group continued.)

The facilitator leaving

The facilitator may leave for a number of reasons. In planned endings, we will consider what are generally thought to be more positive reasons for the facilitator leaving, such as, deciding at a review, or a change of job or role. More negative or painful reasons will be considered in the section on unplanned endings.

In a group that has been running for a long time it is important to ask whether a change in facilitator would be helpful. If this is a usual question in a review, it guards against the question being as a negative reaction to a particular frustration or conflict in the group. Although advocating that it is important to ask the question, we do not advocate that a team should necessarily change their facilitator. If they value the group and it works well, why should they? A new facilitator may offer a valuable new perspectives and ideas, but remaining with the usual facilitator is a safe and reliable option. As in any relationship, the facilitator who is thought to be safe and useful is likely to be asked to remain. Given that staff support groups are difficult enough to sustain, change for its own sake is unlikely to outweigh the pragmatic advantages of a safe and useful group.

The facilitator who leaves because of a change of role or job usually causes uncertainty and disappointment. Despite this the group members tend to accept the decision and recognize it as a normal part of someone's working life. In this case, it is less likely to arouse the anxiety that he or she is leaving because the group has done something to make them go. The facilitator has to both maintain the aim of the group, and facilitate the group acknowledgement about his or her leaving. Negotiating a period of notice, we suggest not less than one month, and reminding them of how many weeks are left, naturally produces a conversation about the facilitator leaving, although this should not take over from the aim of the group. In a valued staff support group, staff may find it difficult to express their dissatisfactions, and it is important the facilitator can ask whether there are any, and be attentive to what may be said, and aware of what is more difficult to say.

Part of leaving is to help the group think whether they want the group to continue, and if so, with whom. Group members typically struggle to think about this, but inquiring about their progress and offering help to find someone, facilitates the process. Sometimes it is helpful to encourage them into action, rather than just facilitate.

Example

The facilitator of a staff support group that had been running for a number of years announced she was leaving because she had been offered a new job. She gave three months' notice. The group members valued the group and were disappointed about the change. The members continued to use the group as normal, with a little time in most sessions discussing what the change would mean for them. The time devoted to this increased as the facilitator's leaving date approached. The usual work continued for part of the sessions, except for the final one, which was devoted to thanking the facilitator and reminiscing about the group and the impact it had. The facilitator discussed with the group members how to approach a new facilitator. There were a number of separate conversations with the commissioner of the group and in this case, the facilitator approached a number of people who may have been interested and able to take over the group. Interested parties were asked to contact the commissioner directly to discuss it further, and to arrange an appointment process.

The discussion between the facilitator, the group and the commissioner concerned logistical information, time of group, people's availability, fees etc, and importantly the right person. The fit of the facilitator is determined by the relevant qualification, and experience, but also their capacity to empathise with and validate the group members' experience. This is not at the cost of being unable to challenge the group. The number of people doing this work is small, and often the facilitator's personal knowledge of how other people work is an important part of appointing someone who will fit with a team.

Notice of loss of funding

We have included loss of funding in planned ending because most organisations that re-allocate funding as a result of financial pressures, warn the relevant parties in advance. With warning, the facilitator has in effect a notice period to discuss how they have found the group, and the impact of the decision on them. It may be that the group can continue perhaps with a facilitator already employed by the organisation.

Example

The group had been running for five months on a busy ward in an independent sector medium secure unit. A new financial year and budget review resulted in a decision that the cost of an external facilitator was too high. His contract was terminated with one month's notice and he was to be replaced with someone employed by the hospital.

The main themes of this group had been the intense anxiety generated by working under a constant threat of assault or responding to clients' severe self-harm. Staff were matter of fact about their work. It was part of the job! This and a macho culture, in the facilitator's view, affected attendance. The facilitator was left with little choice but to accept the decision, like the group members who had little choice but to accept their working conditions or leave their jobs. The closure of the group represented a concrete response that offered an immediate solution to financial pressures. This mirrored the preferred way of working by the team – reflecting on their work was not familiar, or in this case wanted. The facilitator who in effect was sacked, was left feeling hard done to, and out of control, a resource to be used or not. This mirrored the group members' experience of being managed by their organisation. There was little scope to discuss how those who did attend the group felt about the ending, or what an internal facilitator would be like. However, the notice period allowed those who regularly attended to discuss with the facilitator what they did value about the group and make a case for its future structure and aims. This was influential when the facilitator met with the commissioner to discuss the future of the group and its facilitator. In some cases this is the best outcome that can be achieved, when faced with pressures beyond the facilitator's control.

UNPLANNED OR IMPOSED ENDINGS

Poor attendance

A painful ending is when numbers reduce so much that the group is unworkable. Working with less than four members for anything more than a few weeks is not practical. The pressure on group members to fill the time is great, and causes anxiety and guilt. They feel responsible not to let the facilitator and each other down, and resentful that their colleagues have left them to it. These feelings may be manageable if people attend very regularly, but in most cases, this is not possible. It is important that the facilitator has in mind what is the minimum membership that can be worked with. If attempts to increase numbers have failed, warning that the group will close, and proposing a notice period is appropriate. The facilitator should be aware of his or her own feelings about low numbers. It can feel rejecting, and a slow painful end. To close the group if it is only to alleviate the facilitator's feelings, will reduce his or her ability to work with the cause of the problem. Not to respond is to struggle heroically and deny the inevitable.

Example

A staff support group running for a few months with a one year contract struggled to get more than two or three people attending. The group was for staff working in a residential setting with clients who have learning difficulties, many with severe behavioural problems. The facilitator and group members made strenuous efforts, but in vain, to increase membership. The facilitator often wondered about closing the group, but could not bring himself to discuss it. He did not want to let the group members down who did attend: in part because they obviously valued the group, and in part because he would have felt a failure. The team consisted of a core of experienced and dedicated staff, who did not attend the sessions. They were constantly in demand to cover shifts and sort out problems. They were seen as the ones who coped and could be relied on. The staff who attended the group tended to be newer and more junior. They had higher rates of sickness and turnover. As a result their attendance at the group was affected. Recruitment to the unit was problematic, and this coupled with absence problems, meant that there was no one to attend many sessions. It was not unusual for the facilitator to turn up and find that no one was going to attend. Despite this being an ongoing problem he did not terminate the group.

The facilitator felt angry and taken for granted, as if he was expected to put up with anything, and this was an expectation with which he colluded. He wanted to survive and go beyond a culture of always coping. In fact, by not being defeated like the core group of staff, a myth of always coping was perpetuated. The facilitator struggled to acknowledge the pain and rejection that he felt at the poor membership and being unable to change the group's culture. After a period of several sessions with no one attending, he was forced to acknowledge his limitations and those of the group and resign. Reflecting on his decision, he felt he had been desperate to be good enough like the core staff. This was at the expense of working with the wider team to consider how their heroic status affects inexperienced and junior staff and their problems with retention. The facilitator may have more readily discussed this with the unit's commissioner and managers had he been more in touch with his own fear of failure and need to survive at all costs. The discussion would have been about attendance problems, but inevitably the split between those who did and did not attend the group would have been central to it. A formulation of why this occurred may have influenced attendance at the group and allowed for the team dynamic to change as the heroes could begin to be less heroic and less difficult to live up to.

Change of attitude to the staff support group

A new manager, commissioner, or rapid turnover of the staff can result in the staff support group not being wanted and little investment in the original reason it was commissioned. If the facilitator meeting new managers has not worked, or new staff are not willing to attend the group it is likely to close. All staff support groups depend on the support of their organisation. Unsupported, the members naturally feel angry and let down, as may the facilitator. Even unsympathetic managers will usually negotiate a notice period with the facilitator, who should actively pursue this and not feel trampled on and not sink into doing nothing. The feelings of the members are hard to bear. It is easy to join with them against an external enemy. The facilitator and group members can use the notice period to review what worked, and did not work in the group, and to think how other forms of support may be accessed. To join together against the external enemy, is to inhibit thinking, and risk destructive splitting of the staff support group members from their organisation.

Sudden withdrawal of funding

Closely linked to changes in attitudes to the staff support group, or as a result of reorganisation of budgets, or reduced income, the impact of sudden withdrawal of funding is the same; closure. Negotiating a notice period, if at all possible, is important. Whether, and to what extent to resist these issues will be discussed later in the chapter.

Example
A new manager takes over a unit with a staff support group that has been running for a few months and is gradually becoming established. The manager decides that the group should close because staff support will be achieved through individual clinical supervision and mentoring.

Members of the group and the facilitator are angry. There has not been any consultation, the decision was communicated by email, including to the facilitator. The facilitator requests a meeting with the new manager but an appointment is not offered. Such is the level of attack felt by the group and the lack of communication that group members are bewildered and feel impotent. The facilitator and group members are united in their anger, and anxiety. The facilitator, for a time at least, is only reacting to the decision of the organisation and not seeing the broader picture. The group has been given a month's notice and there is little time to respond. The anger turns to resentment and impotency. The facilitator manages to rouse himself from the morass of feelings and contacts the original commissioner of the group who is senior to the new manager. Unfortunately, the group members are not able to move from resentment and feelings of being done to, so do not support the facilitator. Not surprisingly, the manager and commissioner have jointly taken the decision to close the group. The case put by the facilitator is seen as partisan and does not make a difference. The facilitator has to tolerate that the group members, who feel overwhelmed, are not in a position to make a case to the commissioner. The group closes. The anger and disappointment is huge. Nevertheless, the facilitator pushes the membership to review the group and a final report is written to the manager and commissioner, which makes a case that closure of the group was a loss and premature. The report predicts what the impact of closure will be on the team, and makes recommendations for how to communicate decisions more appropriately.

Burnout of the facilitator

McGowan in Chapter 9 describes clearly how the facilitator can be affected by the group. It is ironic that by being emotionally available to the group and listening to their feelings the facilitator is vulnerable to being overcome by his or her own emotions. This is the same dilemma the workers are caught up in, and vulnerable to. There are occasions that facilitators, like the group members, struggle to maintain 'a position between inside and outside . . . and enact what is projected rather than managing it' (Obholzer and Roberts 2006: 137). In doing so, the overwhelming feelings may cause the facilitator to close the group because they feel, or they are, unable to continue. A staff support group in an organisation that causes its members stress because of working with highly disturbed or destructive behaviour is itself vulnerable to being overwhelmed with anxiety. The facilitator of such a group is also vulnerable to the 'dangers of contagion' (Moylan 2006: 51). Closing the group is only appropriate if the facilitator is unable to continue, but effective supervision reduces the likelihood of it, by supporting the facilitator.

Burnout of the facilitator is included in unplanned endings because it is not usually anticipated that the facilitator will feel overwhelmed by their feelings and have to close the group, and at least move on and be replaced.

It is more usually anticipated that the facilitator will be the one who does cope, and make sense of what they are experiencing.

Example

A number of the previous illustrations describe the impact on the facilitator. This example will give more detail. It is of someone facilitating a staff support group for a team in a residential unit working with self-injuring women. The facilitator was employed by the same organisation as the team. He had an explicit role to develop staff support systems. He was receiving monthly supervision from a supervisor also working in the same organisation. The group had been meeting for about a year and was well attended, particularly by a core of members, including the unit manager. There was a suicide on the unit, which had a devastating impact on the staff. Investigations concluded that despite evidenced good practice, the suicide could have been avoided. The feelings in the staff group were of intense guilt and responsibility, and anger that despite their good practice they had been found wanting.

Attendance at the group gradually began to suffer as staff began to implement recommendations to improve their procedures. Feelings of resentment, and anxiety steadily increased. The facilitator came away from sessions feeling overwhelmed with the impact of the staff's feelings. He (the facilitator) felt terribly sorry for the staff, who he thought had been doing their best. He felt it was impossible to relieve them of their guilt, which in turn made him feel guilty. As he struggled with his own reactions and the group members' feelings, he began to dread going to the group. He struggled to know what to say. The group experienced more frequent and longer silences that he was powerless to change. The facilitator knew his guilt and powerlessness were what the group members were also feeling. He knew his impulse to avoid the group was to protect himself from the feelings and his own impotency. His knowledge helped him to continue to go to the group and avoid finding, or accepting, reasons to do other things.

The group members who were attending less because of implementing new procedures, spoke more about their anger with the organisation at making them do extra work, and spoke less and less about their feelings about the suicide. This gradually made the group feel it was losing its way and its value. The facilitator, increasingly desperate to help people with their feelings and save them, became increasingly impotent and much less active in the group. He gradually began to find reasons not to attend.

The group members, and their organisation, were looking for procedures in order to manage their feelings about the suicide. Although it is important to examine procedures and learn from incidents, it can be at the cost of failing to acknowledge people's feelings – the procedures may be used as social defences, and giving an omnipotent sense of protection against the anxiety and guilt that the inevitable occasional failure causes. (How often do investigations and reports say 'this must never happen again', but inevitably it does.)

The facilitator eventually closed the group, because of a combination of his own powerlessness to help its members and finding reasons not to be there. Likewise, the group members increasingly did not use the group to support one another with their feelings, but avoided them by either non-attendance or focusing on new practices and procedures. The facilitator in this example was more vulnerable to enacting the feelings in the group, because he was also a member of the organisation that the suicide happened in. He was vulnerable (as was his supervisor) to the effect of suicide on the whole organisation. Could he have coped better? Could he have maintained a position between the inside and the outside? That he started not to go to the group, in spite of his knowledge suggests not, and that he like the workers was overcome by his emotions.

WORKING WITH ENDINGS

Apart from the desirability of a notice period there is no formula for working with the ending. What to do depends on the circumstances, the group membership and the state of mind of the facilitator. Craib (1994: 28) discussing bereavement says, 'if grieving by the book did not deal with the problem of loss, then nothing could, and however hard we try, in the end nothing can'. Craib was in an experiential training group for therapists who were critical of a group therapist continuing to work following a bereavement. The lesson is not to impose on the staff support group members how they should feel, but to respect their ways of coping with the ending. A long enough notice period gives time for the facilitator to wonder what feelings may not be being expressed and to tentatively make suggestions. However, such is the symbolism and metaphor of the ending of a group, particularly one that has been valued, that dormant, or ignored feelings about loss can be raised. It is not a therapy group, and feelings other than those directly connected with the group can be acknowledged but not explored. It can be a temptation for the facilitator to discuss in depth a group member's personal disclosures. Facilitators are particularly vulnerable to this if they are feeling a sense of disappointment or failure about the ending, and may use it as emotional compensation, to make them feel useful and on familiar territory.

A necessary and adaptive development after loss, is what to do next. The facilitator may have to help the group members think about how to cope without a group, or to find a new facilitator. The balance is important here. To urgently find a replacement structure or facilitator can be a defence against the loss. To have little or no sense of urgency may be to narcissistically idealise the facilitator and the group, and to deny a good enough alternative.

Example

The facilitator told a group that had been running for a number of years that she was leaving in three months time. The group members were shocked and disappointed. Almost immediately they began to ask whether the group would continue, and how they would find a new facilitator. The facilitator said little, other than to acknowledge their shock, and agree to their request to help to find a new facilitator. Over the coming weeks, the group continued as usual, apart from occasional references to the pending departure of the facilitator. The group members were reminded when there were eight weeks remaining by asking them what information they wanted to find a replacement facilitator. There followed a thoughtful discussion of what they valued in a facilitator, and what the potential appointment process would be. The facilitator's advice was asked about how to approach people. This advice was largely ignored until some time after she left, and the team did not organise finding a replacement. Simply by asking how things were going the facilitator prompted the group to keep in mind their feelings, and draw their own conclusions about their lack of activity. In the final two sessions ordinary work was spontaneously partially suspended, to look back over the life and development of the group and what had and had not worked well. The team having expressed their feelings, with a prompt from the facilitator (to give permission to move on from loss), continued by discussing recent events in their work. They appointed a new facilitator within two months of the former one leaving.

Working with endings resulting from disappointment in the group

If a review concludes that a group has not been useful, the group members are likely to feel the facilitator has been a disappointment. Equally, the facilitator is likely to experience the group members as disappointing, or be disappointed in himself or herself. One of the most difficult situations is when the group is blamed for causing difficulties between group members and their organisation.

Pines (1991: 112) writing about clients who stay in group analysis for a long time says, 'the timing of leaving a group may be appropriate or may be premature; which applies should become clear in the working out process'.

This is in part why a long enough notice period is useful. If there is disappointment in the group then understanding why there is, is important. The unspoken and unrecognized reasons for requesting a staff support group discussed earlier in the book may contribute to this. If the stated aim was to support staff with an aspect of their work, but the covert reason was to address team conflict and poor management (see Chapter 2), then disappointment that the covert aim was not achieved may be expressed by saying that nothing has changed. Even at this late stage, it may be possible for the real reasons the group was wanted to be spoken about. What to do next can then be discussed. The role of the facilitator is to help the group consider whether it will be possible for them to work on the issue in the future. If the ending is 'premature', it may be that only the unspoken aim has not been achieved. It may be an 'appropriate' ending, because to have addressed the real issue would have been too threatening and destructive. Whatever the capacity of the group members and the facilitator to analyse the reasons for their disappointment, their feelings should be heard and 'attended to' (Moylan 2006: 53).

Disappointment in the facilitation is difficult for the facilitator to bear. Often it is about their style or attitude. If another group is wanted, their disappointment in the facilitator gives important information about an alternative approach that they may have found more helpful. Sometimes a group and a facilitator just do not fit together.

In our experience, it is common that if a staff support group does end prematurely then it is prognostic of what future difficulties they are likely to have with a new facilitator. By identifying what went wrong and how it may be addressed gives a future group a better chance of success. It may be necessary for the facilitator to predict any future difficulties particularly if the group members are struggling to think about what went wrong and why.

Whether to oppose external threats to close the group

External threats to close staff support groups usually come from new managers, regimes or corporate climates and decisions, as well as other scenarios described in this chapter. The members of a staff support group and the facilitator may not have information that has influenced a decision to close a group. Managers may have made a decision that is unpopular, but they are likely to have decided to close a group because they believe it to be in the best interests of the organisation or group members.

Whether to resist an attempt to close a group is a decision taken jointly by the facilitator and the group members, although it is the opinion of the group members that takes precedence. The facilitator is there to help them to explore the influences and dynamics affecting their decision – e.g. passivity or being too overtly resistant. Group members and the facilitator are vulnerable to feeling rejected and disappointed and passive acceptance can be a consequence. A proactive approach that appraises the situation and the reasons for the decision protects against passively accepting closure and can help the group members decide whether they think the decision should or can be opposed. The facilitator's ability to influence the decision will be influenced by their relationship with the organisation (as an external or insider facilitator) and by their own personal reaction which is something to explore with their supervisor.

The final report

Whether the group has ended by mutual consent or external imposition, a final written report to the commissioner of the group can provide a valuable guide to future thinking about staff support groups and organisational influences that affect them. The report could include how long the group has been running, average and range of attendance, the group's aims and the extent to which they were achieved with particular successes and failures, and identifying obstacles and difficulties that hindered the group, with recommendations for what would help any future group.

Ending the relationship with the facilitator

This book states staff support groups are not therapy groups; that is not to say they are not therapeutic or that processes that occur in therapy do not occur in staff support groups. For some members their relationship with the facilitator will be extremely important to them. They may have experienced being heard and validated for the first time in their lives. Observing the facilitator at work may have influenced their career path. Simply to have experienced being vulnerable and feeling safe may be momentous. Unlike in some therapy groups, individual members will not have had a chance to explore their relationship with the facilitator. The facilitator is likely to be aware of their importance, but not fully understand why. Craib (1994: 28) says, 'in the end it is up to each of us to find our own metaphors and places for grief'. For those group members for whom the facilitator has been emotionally important, the task is that it can be said, and a little of why it was so. As with valued colleagues leaving a team, their value is acknowledged, but not what they represent to someone. Their worth is taken at face value. A group member may transfer positive or negative feelings towards the facilitator that originated from their relationship with someone else, usually a family member. However, this should not be explored or resolved. It is up to the individual, as Craib says, to find their own way of grieving, which may include little acknowledgement, of any significance.

As with therapy groups, because of the potential for unresolved issues, future contact between the facilitator and group members should be avoided, or if this is not possible, boundaried as part of a professional network. The facilitator has influence and power. Care should be taken when a group ends that this is not used to inappropriately influence former group members. The advice to most professionals is not to have relationships with their clients. In this case, facilitators' 'clients' are often colleagues, and those relationships need to be boundaried and material discussed in the group kept confidential.

Facilitators are likely to have disclosed little personal information while they have been involved in the group. Group members will ask, like with colleagues, where they are going and what they will do next. Answering questions about their professional lives can be helpful and normalise the relationship and ending. Our recommendation is to keep any conversation in the professional and out of the personal domain.

CONCLUSION

Staff support groups can end in planned and unplanned ways. Even with unplanned and disappointing endings, the process of closing the group can be helpful. There should be if at all possible a notice period that is negotiated with the group members. Their feelings about the ending need hearing and validating. Any underlying reasons influencing the ending, should if possible be recognized. The ability of the facilitator to hear the group members' feelings and the underlying reasons for a group closing, are significantly influenced by their ability to recognize the difference between what they are made to feel by the group and what are their own feelings. A staff group ending can be very significant for some members and not for others. People need to be helped to react in their own way and not in a way the facilitator may think best.

Chapter 8

Do staff support groups work?

David Kennard and Phil Hartley

The apparently simple question of the title is no easier to answer than its better known siblings, 'does psychotherapy work?', 'does counselling work?' and 'do groups work?' As with other members of this family of questions, the answer is of more than academic interest. The arrival of evidence-based practice has ensured that funding decisions for psychological therapies are strongly influenced, if not determined, by evidence of their effectiveness. Staff support groups are not for patients and do not come under the searching gaze of the National Institute for Health and Clinical Excellence, but in an age of evidence-based practice it seems appropriate to apply the same test, and to ask what evidence there is for the effectiveness of staff support groups.

Our first step was to look for what research has been done on this question, starting with *Google Scholar* and following up all the relevant references. We were not optimistic we would find very much, as most of the little that has been written about staff support groups reflects the personal experience and accumulated practice wisdom of practitioners. However, our search of material going back over the past two decades discovered 12 studies that had attempted a systematic evaluation of some kind, either of one or more staff support groups or of the experiences of mental health professionals of sources of support where one of these was a staff support group. We restricted our search mainly to studies that referred explicitly to staff support groups but included two other studies. One was an evaluation of 'reflection groups' that were defined very much as we would define staff support groups, and the other was where the author stated that during the course of his ongoing study he decided to change the name from staff support groups to 'professional development groups' in order to encourage staff to take responsibility for their own professional development.

The studies used a wide range of methods: experimental design comparing wards with and without a staff support group, post-group interviews, questionnaire evaluations of groups taking place in everyday practice, surveys of staff experiences of support systems that included staff groups and reviews of the literature on staff support groups.

We believe we have been able to locate enough studies to identify some general conclusions. Perhaps the most important is that some staff find support groups helpful and some do not, and that the salient question is not whether staff support groups in general are effective, but what the characteristics are of successful groups, who finds them helpful and who doesn't, and what factors influence this. We also found, contrary to the convention that 'hard' data provides the best evidence of effectiveness, that those studies that interviewed people about their experiences provided the most useful and telling evidence of the benefits and drawbacks of staff support groups. In what follows we summarise each study in turn and then discuss what can be learned from the accumulated evidence.

EXPERIMENTAL STUDIES

Le Blanc *et al.* (2007) undertook a huge study across 29 oncology wards in the Netherlands, in which 9 wards were randomly selected for what was described as 'a team-based burnout intervention programme . . . that included support group meetings in which care providers were able to share their work-related feelings and to discuss work-related problems and ways of solving them' (Le Blanc *et al.* 2007: 215). Two hundred and sixty staff on the experimental wards and 404 staff on the 20 control wards were asked to complete a series of questionnaires before and after the six months experiment and again six months later. The programme itself consisted of six three-hour 'training sessions' at monthly intervals, which comprised a mix of structured education and active problem-solving to cope with work stressors. Self-report measures focused on emotional exhaustion and depersonalisation as two key aspects of burnout. The study found that staff on the experimental wards experienced significantly less emotional exhaustion and depersonalisation than the control wards at the end of the programme, and that this difference continued at follow-up for emotional exhaustion, although the absolute differences between the wards was small. Interestingly it also found that differences between individuals were greater than differences over time, and that 'there appeared to be considerable intra-individual stability for exhaustion and depersonalisation' (Le Blanc *et al.* 2007: 220). In other words – although the technical reporting of the data is almost impenetrable – the implication is that although the programme made some difference, individuals tended to stay as they were.

Ritter *et al.* (1995) reported a small-scale experiment of running six three-hour sessions of an 'intensive social support group' twice weekly for 7 psychiatric nurses on one ward, comparing the outcome with two control groups – 7 nurses from the same ward who didn't take part in the group, and 11 nurses in another hospital ward. Outcome measures were five questionnaires, including the General Health Questionnaire (GHQ), given at the start and six to eight weeks later. The most striking finding was on the GHQ scores of the group members, the number of nurses whose scores indicated psychiatric 'caseness' falling from six to two. No changes were found in the other ward but an interesting finding was that improvements on most of the measures occurred in both sets of nurses on the ward with the group – nurses who didn't attend the group appeared to benefit from the presence of the group on their ward. The authors suggest that this was 'possibly a result of being directly affected by their colleagues' new outlook on their job and its difficulties' (Ritter *et al.* 1995: 174).

POST-GROUP INTERVIEWS

We included the following study of reflection groups for nurses on two psychiatric wards (one general, one elderly) mainly because the interview method yielded a number of useful pointers to what is helpful or hindering in staff support groups. Olofsson (2005) described the study as a means of providing support in relation to the use of coercion. The group sessions were guided by questions such as 'What happened during the incident when coercion was used?', 'How did it feel?', 'In what other ways could we have acted?' From the point of view of this book, the study was limited by its specific focus and also by the small numbers in the groups and the brevity of attendance – each session was attended by two to four nurses, with most attending only one session. Nevertheless the research interview format allowed participants to identify a number of benefits of this kind of group. These included:

- being able to express their own feelings on a more personal level than in other clinical supervision groups;
- recognizing themselves in other members' experiences, no longer feeling alone, feeling more confident and secure in their work;
- gaining new perspectives and new awareness of others' ideas on the use of coercion;
- sharing fellowship with colleagues, developing greater awareness of the needs of colleagues and students, opening the way for more care of each other;
- relating more effectively with patients: gaining a better understanding of both their own and patients' actions.

The negative aspects of the groups identified were mainly to do with the particular focus of the study:

- meetings did not occur in close proximity to an incident;
- participants wanted to talk about a wider range of issues;
- some participants had no problem using coercion.

The study also identified a number of factors that could influence the value of such groups (Olofsson 2005: 264–5). These included the following.

- The relationship between the group leader and participants, which 'determines whether the supervision has a restorative effect or constitutes an additional stressor for the participants'. (We take Olofsson's use of the term supervision to be broad enough to include staff support groups.)
- The importance of voluntary participation: 'When one is pressured or forced to reflect, reflection will not necessarily be a fruitful experience.'
- Nurses were conscious that 'their need for supervision and support could be assumed by colleagues as indicating that they could not manage their job'.
- Support and encouragement from 'committed, enthusiastic clinical managers'.
- Who else attended the group: 'individuals choose who they want to confide in – they may not choose to confide in the people in the group'.

In a much earlier study Booth and Faulkner (1986) set up short-term support groups for nurses in five district general hospitals – two focused on helping nurses to give up smoking and three for 'general support'. The report gives limited information, but it appears that 39 nurses attended the general support groups at least once, with an average attendance of 3 or 4. The take-up in the different hospitals varied enormously. In one hospital the group appears to have met only once, in another it ran for an agreed six sessions, whereas in the third it was set up for 8 weeks but continued for 16 weeks and the nurse members then carried it on themselves. Strangely the authors do not discuss any possible reasons for these differences, although there are hints in their reported findings.

All 39 members completed a questionnaire at the start and most were interviewed after the groups were completed. Almost all said they found the groups beneficial for the discussion of professional problems and a third said they also benefited from other aspects of personal development. However, the interviews and a questionnaire survey in one of the hospitals identified some common concerns about the groups that may have kept people away. These included worries about breaches of confidence, distrust of nurses in different grades, and a view that 'nurses don't need help'. One nurse said she felt upset 'when a senior colleague had referred in public to aspects of the group's meeting in spite of assurances of confidentiality given during the sessions'. A student nurse said she was afraid she might say something that would lead others to think, 'What's wrong with her? Can't she cope? What is she doing in this job?' (Booth and Faulkner 1986: 249). This was a study of general hospital nursing more than 20 years ago; it would be interesting to know if anything has changed.

EVALUATION OF STAFF SUPPORT GROUPS IN EVERYDAY PRACTICE

In some ways these are the most useful studies, the ones that explore what has been termed 'effectiveness' rather than 'efficacy' – the former being what happens in everyday practice rather than under research conditions. We found three studies, each using a different method.

Nancy Tommasini (1992) was a psychiatric consultation liaison nurse invited by the head nurse of a specialty unit in her hospital to 'provide assistance in decreasing conflict and improving communication among staff'. She proposed a series of weekly staff support group meetings that would be evaluated using the Work Environment Scale (WES) (Moos 1986) before and after 12 sessions. Not only did this provide an objective basis for looking at the effects of the group, Tommasini also shared the initial results at the first meeting. She found this 'appeared to serve as a non-threatening way of approaching sensitive issues such as supervisor support', and that staff requested a particular WES dimension as the topic for the week.

She also found immediate evidence of communication problems in the group – e.g. members talking to each other in a 'critical, disparaging manner' – and was able to 'model the provision of positive feedback as well calling attention to negative aspects of their communication styles' (Tommasini 1992: 43).

Results showed significant changes on two of the ten WES dimensions – increases in Clarity (the extent to which workers know what to expect) and in Control (the extent to which management uses rules to keep employees under control). Tommasini also observed improvements in how staff communicated with each other, and members brought back examples to the group of how they had worked out a problematic issue on the unit. After 12 sessions members felt there was more work to be done and requested to continue the group.

What we particularly liked about this study was using evaluation measures as part of the work but still putting the needs of the team first. We were struck by the collaborative approach, and the way the group's problems were demonstrated in the meetings, enabling the facilitator's interventions to be experienced as responding to the needs of the group.

Another approach to evaluating staff support groups in everyday practice is periodically to ask all the members to complete a feedback questionnaire. This was the method used by Thomas (1995, 2001, 2003) in relation to a number of groups he has facilitated in mental health services, both ward-based and in the community. This has the advantage of being adaptable to a changing staff population (which would make Tommasini's before and after method difficult), but can suffer from a lower response rate and the fixed questions that may limit what can be learned from the responses.

In his first study, Thomas (1995) sent a questionnaire to 34 members of five groups he facilitated for district nurses, enrolled nurses and school nurses. Twenty-six (62 per cent) responded, and most of these reported that the groups had helped with patient-related concerns and other work-related concerns. However, only seven felt they had 'gained support from the group', and six said they had made 'developments in self-awareness and in their ability to put feelings into words'. Interestingly the lowest graded nurses gave highest rating to the value of group attendance. The question-naire also asked about disadvantages. Those noted included people being 'left with unresolved feelings at the end of the meeting', 'things discussed not being acted on later', and the group bringing anxieties to the fore. One respondent said that after a group she 'often felt angry and miserable for the remainder of the day'.

Responding to the implications of his findings, Thomas went on to develop a staff support model in which staff support groups were renamed professional development groups and which included individual supervision for team leaders and team building days (Thomas 2001). The groups were renamed with the aim of getting staff to take responsibility for their learning, as Thomas believed that the concept of support may indicate a passive role for the participant. We confess to some scepticism about the issue being one of the name, but we do think that the practical changes Thomas introduced along with the name change may well have had a positive effect. These included a written statement of the group goals, and an individual meeting with each new member before they joined the group, in which the aims and commitment were discussed and the member signed a written agreement to maintain the group boundaries.

A subsequent questionnaire evaluation of groups on two acute psy-chiatric wards had an 80 per cent response rate (Thomas 2003). Of these, 84 per cent found groups helpful or very helpful overall. The most highly valued aspects were the group as a diagnostic tool for highlighting issues on the ward (83 per cent) and as a place for debriefing after traumatic incidents (80 per cent). Seventy-five per cent saw it as a helpful means of encouraging communication between staff and 67 per cent for discussing difficult patients. Fewer (58 per cent) felt it was helpful in coping with work stresses and 21 per cent said it was unhelpful in this respect. The same issue as in the earlier study was that 'issues are thrown up that never get resolved'.

We were impressed with Thomas's commitment to evaluating his groups, and to acting on the results – to good effect. Overall these groups seemed to be helpful for many team members, though some members felt they were unhelpful and refused to attend, and unresolved issues still occurred – raising the question of how much these are inevitable and how much they are the attributes of a particular team, group or facilitator.

The third study we include here (Milton and Davison 1997) contains no measures but did set out to ask a very important question – why two staff support groups set up at the same time had very different outcomes. Both groups came from requests to a psychotherapy department for a group facilitator, one from a ward for violent psychotic patients who are returned to the referring ward when they improve (called Unit A), one from a pilot team for a new community-based psychosis service (Unit B). Both groups were preceded by one or more initial consultation meetings with the team, and were then set up for an agreed period of 6 or 12 months. The authors described how on Unit A staff were enthusiastic about the group in the initial consultations but that once started, attendance 'dropped dramatically', most staff came late, and there were never more than one or two disciplines represented at any meeting. On Unit B attendance was high and the group was well used. What could account for such marked differences?

Unit A performed a valuable but unrewarding role for the wider organisation. Patients were unwilling or contemptuous, and the reward for effective care was to lose the patient. The facilitator noted that the staff function of forceful restraint of patients was valued more than 'just talking to patients', and that the group also denigrated talking in favour of action. The facilitator found it a major struggle to connect her own reactions of helplessness and impotent anger with the experience of the staff, and longed for the year to be up. Just occasionally the group entered a thoughtful and concerned mood, which disappeared when the membership changed.

Unit B felt under pressure as a high prestige experimental team, with critical and persecutory relationships, but 'the task of the facilitator was greatly helped by the team members' keen awareness that their work and morale was suffering on account of these difficulties . . . and there was enough hopeful expectation that the facilitator would be helpful that more sceptical members were carried along' (Milton and Davison 1997: 141).

Key differences identified in this study between the less and more successful group were the relationship of the unit with the wider institution – how valued its function was, the nature of the clinical task – whether the feelings aroused can be spoken about, and the combined effect of these two factors and the availability of 'skilled and supportive leadership' on the morale of the team.

SURVEYS OF STAFF EXPERIENCES OF SUPPORT SYSTEMS

A lot of papers and government documents have been written about the needs of staff in mental health services, and there have been a number of attempts to survey the available supports and how well they work. Here we will restrict ourselves to two studies that made specific mention of staff support groups.

Robertson and Davison (1997) reviewed all the groups meeting regularly in one large 450 bed psychiatric teaching hospital. They found a total of 220 groups meeting regularly, of which a third (73) were staff groups. These were a mix of larger multi-disciplinary groups (11–40 members) and smaller mainly single discipline groups (3–10 members). Half the groups had a clearly identified leader, either from outside or from within the group. Others valued a leaderless group as a forum for discussing work-related issues. Using interviews and questionnaires, they found a general lack of clarity about the groups' structure, purpose, functioning and theoretical framework, and that many groups 'served only to increase anxiety or to reflect the anxieties and defences of the units they served', although there were 'notable exceptions' (Milton and Davison 1997: 136).

Reid *et al.* (1999) interviewed 30 mental health staff from three community teams and three wards, about how they coped with work stresses, and their experiences of individual supervision and staff support groups. Not surprisingly, talking to colleagues was given as the most frequent way of coping and other team members as the most important source of support. All but 3 of the 30 had experienced a staff support group. (All the community-based staff had access to a 'psychodynamically facilitated' staff group. Of the three wards, one ward had a facilitated group, one had a group without a facilitator, and on the third a staff group had 'collapsed'.) The interviewers found a fairly even split between 12 whose views were predominantly positive and 15 who were mainly negative in their views on the usefulness of the groups.

The 'positives' described finding it 'useful to have the opportunity to discuss personal or professional difficulties and individual concerns as part of a team'. They said, for example, 'a chance to say how you feel', makes you feel part of the team', 'I feel I can discuss anything that bothers me . . . I feel very supported' (Reid *et al.* 1999: 312).

By contrast the 'negatives' resented the time taken up in a busy schedule and felt the groups were a waste of time. Almost all the senior staff (two team leaders, three ward managers and six medical staff) saw their role as providing support and encouragement to the team and felt it would be 'unhelpful to moan or appear negative'. Other common comments were that people were unsure how to use the support group and felt unsafe discussing their real concerns or anxieties. Two felt intimidated by the size of the group but three felt the group was too poorly attended to be effective.

Suggestions for improving the groups included more consistent attendance, a more structured format, training in how to use groups, and a more active facilitator.

But the most interesting finding was that 'the same staff support group could provoke very different reactions in different individuals' (Reid *et al.* 1999: 312), i.e. positive and negative comments were made by different members of the same group. This seems to us to have important implications for the evaluation of the effectiveness of staff support groups, as well as the role of the facilitator. The question is not, are the groups effective – yes or no – but who are they useful for, and can modifications in the way they are facilitated increase the proportion of staff who find them useful?

LITERATURE REVIEWS OF STAFF GROUPS

Ritter *et al.* (1995) reported a rather cursory review of studies of the efficacy of staff support groups in the book *Stress and Coping in Mental Health Nursing* (Carsin *et al.* 1995). They concluded that 'It has rarely been shown what is required of a staff support group in order for it to be of any use. Most mental health units tend to put a group of staff in a room once a week and expect them to get on with it' (Ritter *et al.* 1995: 169). A decade earlier Kanas (1986) had published a broad review of the literature on staff support groups for mental health staff and trainees. He identified two main types of staff group described in the 1970s and 80s: 'system-oriented' – i.e. ward-based and team-based groups (what we would call staff support groups); and 'member-oriented' – often run on training courses with closed membership – that we would call sensitivity groups. Evidence regarding the effectiveness of the system-oriented groups was generally favourable but anecdotal, while Kanas cautiously concluded that the findings of questionnaire studies 'support the notion that longer-term member-oriented groups are useful for their participants' (Kanas 1986: 287).

Kanas concluded with three key factors influencing the success of support groups for mental health workers.

- Clear and agreed goals.
- An appropriate leadership style – Kanas refers to the leader being more active and transparent, fostering cohesion and universality, reframing issues in terms of common themes, avoiding interpretation but not precluding non-punitive confrontation, and possibly offering advice and guidance.
- The leader also having awareness of general systems theory and how issues in the larger system may be affecting the staff on a unit.

DISCUSSION

The studies described above refer to very different kinds of staff support groups, ranging from short-term structured sessions to staff 'being put in a room and expected to get on with it'. Given this range, it is not surprising that some reviews (Harvey 1992; Ritter *et al.* 1996; Robertson and Davison

1997) found little evidence that staff support groups are effective. On the other hand studies of carefully set up groups that have used before and after measures (Tommasini 1992; Ritter *et al.* 1995; Le Blanc *et al.* 2007) have found small but significant changes in the direction of the groups' aims.

The finding by Reid *et al.* (1999) that members of the same group can have different experiences, some positive and some negative, seems to present a strong argument against relying on average or pooled results to evaluate staff support groups. If members divide fairly equally into those who do and who don't find the group useful, the overall picture of little or no benefit is likely to mask the true and more important situation – that some members find staff groups very helpful and some find them unhelpful, unsafe or a waste of time.

Just as we would not reject a treatment that was effective for half the population but want to ask who it does and does not work for, so our response to these findings is to rephrase the question in the title as:

- What are the characteristics of staff who find staff support groups helpful?
- What are the characteristics of staff who find staff support groups unhelpful?
- Are there characteristics of a team or unit that favour or work against staff finding a staff support group helpful?
- Can staff support groups be modified to increase the proportion of staff who find them helpful?

What are the characteristics of staff who find staff support groups helpful?

Drawing on the findings of the studies we found, and bearing in mind these studies are often small and that such findings are tentative, it appears that – other things being equal – staff who benefit from support groups are those who value and seek out the following opportunities:

- improving communication between staff;
- being able to express feelings on a personal level;
- feeling less alone;
- gaining new awareness from others' ideas;
- gaining greater awareness of the needs of one's colleagues;
- being able to discuss patient-related concerns and gain a better understanding of their own and patients' actions.

The finding that lower grades of staff tend to rate staff support groups higher is consistent with the above list, since several items may be particularly helpful for staff who feel themselves to be nearer the periphery of the team.

What are the characteristics of staff who find staff support groups unhelpful?

The studies we looked at suggested the following attributes are associated with finding staff support groups unhelpful.

- Staff in senior clinical or management roles who feel that it would be bad for team morale if they were to 'moan' about things they find difficult or unpleasant.
- Staff who feel intimidated, uncomfortable or unsafe with some aspect(s) of the group – e.g. its size, or other members of the team.
- Staff looking for closure or solutions to problems, who feel frustrated when a problem is left unresolved.
- Staff wishing to avoid anxiety and who feel worse when anxieties are brought to the fore.

There are some important questions raised here. Are senior staff right to be concerned about the potential damage to staff whom they see it as their role to support, if they were to share their own concerns? Would the rest of the team value their honesty, or would they prefer not to know? Would they be better role models for appearing resilient and unflappable, or for showing their vulnerable side? The likely answer is that different members of the team need different things from the senior staff, and that both approaches – acting positive or sharing difficulties – will be valued by some but not all staff. In a well-functioning group, discussion of this very question would be a good way forward. This is a complex issue and we discuss elsewhere the pros and cons of managers attending a staff support group.

The problem of some staff feeling intimidated or unsafe is probably the most common in many staff groups, and may arise out of a combination of the individual's 'internal world' and the dynamics of the group. By internal world we mean the predisposition to see other people in general as friendly or hostile. The person who anticipates hostility will not find any group situation easy. With encouragement and support this may change very gradually, and there may not be a lot the facilitator can do in the short term. Lack of safety arising from the dynamics of the group is however very much within the facilitator's remit – e.g. to comment if one member or a subgroup is dominating the group, and ensure everyone has a chance to speak if they want to.

The two other negatives – frustration at unresolved problems and bringing anxieties to the surface – are, unfortunately for some, intrinsic to most staff support groups, and are best dealt with by clarifying this in the aims of the group. Teams often include a wide range of personalities – doers and thinkers, the resilient and the fragile. The more the staff group can encompass this range the more use it can be to the whole team, which requires team members to tolerate and even value their differences.

Are there characteristics of a team/unit that favour or work against staff finding a staff support group useful?

Much of this book has been devoted to identifying and dealing with aspects of a team or organisation that may undermine a staff support group. Surprisingly we found only two research studies that touched on this important issue (Booth and Faulkner 1986; Milton and Davison 1997) – perhaps because it is dealt with more in the clinical and theoretical literature. The lessons to be drawn from these studies are that staff will be reluctant to use a staff support group when:

- there is mistrust of colleagues, particularly those in senor positions who are present in the group;
- the confidentiality of the group is not trusted;
- there is a prevailing view that to be seen to take part in such a group is a sign that you are not up to the job;
- the work of the team is not felt to be valued by the wider organisation;
- there is a prevailing culture that elevates action above 'just talking'.

Can staff support groups be modified to increase the proportion of staff who find them helpful?

It is often said, as we have done elsewhere in the book, that staff support groups are not for everyone – hence the common recommendation that they should be voluntary. But is this inevitable, or are there approaches a facilitator can take to address at least some of the unhelpful aspects outlined above and generally to enhance the benefits of the group? The studies we looked at came up with a large number of factors that were cited as influences on the benefits of the group.

At the start

- Agreeing the aims and boundaries with members.
- A preparatory meeting of each new member with the facilitator to clarify the nature and purpose of group, emphasising personal responsibility for using the group as a learning experience. This may also help to identify and discuss any potential negative views or expectations.
- The facilitator sharing with the group the results of evaluation measures.

In the group

- An active facilitator style – e.g. asking questions, giving feedback on the effects of communication within the group, monitoring how safe the group feels to the members.
- Building a positive, trusting relationship between the members and the facilitator, who affirms members' thought and feelings. (It was noted in one study that this relationship could impact on whether the group has a restorative effect or constitutes an additional stressor.)
- Encouraging members to report back to the group any benefits occurring between sessions.

Factors outside the group the facilitator should be aware of as having an influence on how well the group functions

- The level of support and encouragement of managers/team leaders.
- Views of non-attending staff e.g. if they see the need for support indicating that staff can't mange their job.
- Relationship with the wider organisation or society at large – is the team's task widely valued or is it seen as a 'dustbin' role?

We would not wish to claim that the benefits of staff support groups can be made universal. However, we would argue that the dislike of such groups by around half of care staff is not immutable and that it is very much worth the effort to try out ways of facilitating staff support groups that increase their value.

Some comments on outcome measures

'Hard' data

Some commentators on research methods have suggested that the proper indicators of success for staff support groups are so-called 'hard' data such as staff sickness rates, retention and turnover, and the frequency of recorded violent or adverse incidents (Milton and Davison 1997; Haigh 2000). None of the studies we found used these measures, and we would suggest that had they done so they would have told us little. Such measures would be far too easily affected by events beyond the influence of a staff support group – e.g. an influenza epidemic, the age of the staff or different individual thresholds for recording an incident as adverse.

As a good general principle, the choice of outcome measure should reflect as closely as possible the aims of the group. A group set up to improve staff communication should select or develop a measure of staff communication. A group set up to help staff cope with work stress or traumatic incidents should select measures of the impact of these. And if a group *was* set up to reduce staff sickness absence, then this would indeed be an appropriate outcome measure.

Questionnaires

Questionnaires and rating scales rely on the self-report of individuals. They include standardised measures such as the Ward Atmosphere Scale and Work Environment Scale (Moos 1997) and questionnaires developed by the researcher for their particular project.

The advantage, and lure, of well-developed standard self-report measures is that they have comparative norms for different populations, known reliability and validity, and ambiguous or biased wording has been ironed out. The disadvantage is that they are often too broad to be sensitive to the effects of the group. Even in well-conducted studies such as Tommasini (1992) and Le Blanc *et al.* (2007) the measures only picked up relatively small changes, although we see quite vivid reactions in Tommasini's descriptive report of the group.

An alternative is to design one's own questionnaire, as in Thomas (1995, 2003), though this has its disadvantages. Answers to closed questions are easy to score but may miss vital views, whereas answers to open ended questions can be difficult to summarise. A balance of both types of question may be better – an example developed by one of the authors is shown in Box 8.1. An advantage of a tailored questionnaire is that it has obvious relevance for the group members, and the results can be fed back to the group to encourage a dialogue about its benefits and difficulties.

Interviews

Some of the most useful and telling findings in the studies came from interviews with staff about their experiences of staff support groups (Booth and Faulkner 1986; Olofsson 2005; Reid *et al.* 1999). Although this requires additional resources – it would not be wise for the facilitator to interview his or her own group members – the potential value of getting as close as possible to a true reflection of the group experience make this a very attractive approach. Issues of confidentiality and how the data will be used will be paramount, but the availability of a trainee mental health professional seeking a research project could present a good opportunity to try this approach.

CONCLUSIONS

We have tried to extract the important lessons from the slim number of studies that have used a systematic approach to evaluating the effectiveness of staff support groups. In brief these are as follows.

Box 8.1 Suggested questionnaire items to evaluate a staff support group

[to be completed anonymously]

1. How many meetings of the staff support group have you attended in the past six months?

    None   1–3   more than 3

2. How supportive have you found the meetings to be?

    not at all supportive   1   2   3   4   5   very supportive

3. How much do you feel the meetings have been able to discuss difficult situations?

    not at all   1   2   3   4   5   very fully

4. How constructive do you feel the discussions have been?

    not at all   1   2   3   4   5   very constructive

5. How much do you feel you have been able to learn from listening to others in the group?

    nothing   1   2   3   4   5   a great deal

6. Please mention something that you personally found particularly helpful in the meetings.

7. Please mention something that you have found unhelpful in the meetings.

8. How helpful would you rate the facilitator? Please explain the reasons for your rating.

    not at all helpful   1   2   3   4   5   very helpful

9. Please note anything you feel would improve the meetings.

10. Any further comments? (Please continue comments overleaf if necessary)

1   There is clear evidence that well set up and well run staff support groups are experienced as beneficial.
2   The most successful groups are those set up as a joint undertaking by a staff team that recognizes it has problems, its leader and the facilitator.
3   Even where these ideal conditions do not occur, staff groups with an external facilitator are likely to be experienced as helpful by around half of those taking part.
4   The benefits, and the impediments to these benefits, are well documented. Factors affecting how beneficial the members find a staff support group include personal expectations, role status and the prevailing atmosphere and culture of the workplace.
5   The style of the facilitator is an important factor in influencing how beneficial members find the group.

Research findings always pose new questions so we will end this chapter by identifying some questions raised in this review that point the way to further research on the effectiveness of staff support groups.

- What attributes or attitudes are associated with whether an individual finds staff support groups beneficial or not?
- To what extent can the style of the facilitator increase the number of staff who benefit from a staff support group?
- Are the concerns of some senior staff justified, that showing their feelings to the team will undermine their leadership role or the morale of the team?

PART II

On learning from the short life of a staff support group in an acute admission inpatient mental health setting

Bill McGowan

EDITORS' INTRODUCTION

In this chapter Bill McGowan provides the reader with the honest and revealing diary of a staff group facilitator that highlights a number of the themes and issues discussed in Part I. He illustrates the importance of preliminary negotiations around things like room logistics and group membership (see Chapters 3 and 4), and how a tacit understanding with the unit manager can come unstuck when a membership boundary is crossed. He shows the considerable pressures on the facilitator who struggles to survive and keep the group going (see Chapter 5), and illustrates several of the issues around endings, including the risks to the facilitator of burnout, that we discuss in Chapter 7. McGowan discusses several of these points in his concluding reflections.

This is an account of the birth, short life and death of a support group established for a nursing team working in an acute admission setting in a mental health unit in the South of England. I was approached by a postgraduate mental health nursing student undertaking post-registration studies who wished to incorporate a support group into her strategy for developing a practice-based integrated study. She asked if I would be willing to facilitate a support group for a multi-disciplinary staff team. I had received many such requests before and agreed in principle provided they obtained support from their unit managers. In each case, no one came back.

THE CONTEXT

The nursing team worked in a mental health unit situated at the back of a district general hospital complex. The 26-bedded inpatient ward was situated on the second floor of a three-storey 1960s purpose-built building.

The ground floor housed a day hospital for elderly clients with mental health problems, the first floor housed a six-bedded intensive mental health care ward and the top floor, an administration suite. The nursing team provided what they referred to as integrated, client-centred, humanistic, individualised nursing care. The complement of 22 full-time nursing staff provided 24-hour care working across three shifts, seven days a week. The nursing team also manned a non-funded 24-hour emergency telephone helpline for ex-clients during the evenings, at night and at weekends.

Following my preliminary discussions with the student I gained the impression that the ward was a busy and often difficult place to be whereby the staff struggled courageously to provide non-judgemental care in the face of overwhelming emotional pressures. They did not have a structured line of support but individually sought out trusted colleagues of a similar disposition to whom they could turn. This self-initiated, informal but fragile arrangement enabled some staff to sound out and sound off during times of pressure. This interpersonal osmotic process was helpful for some individuals but often left the way open to the formation of divisive subgroups; the development of splitting among staff; to scapegoating and the development of cliff-hanging unresolved peer conflicts. Invariably, this had a deleterious effect on the socio-emotional atmosphere on the ward and impacted negatively on individual self-esteem, staff relations and client care.

The student felt that a regular support group might help to foster a more egalitarian peer culture of understanding and trust amongst the staff. She believed that it would rein in and contain some of the more negative dynamics acted out between staff and improve the socio-emotional atmosphere on the ward. I noted at the time that in the history of the staff team (as mediated through the student's narrative) there had been a golden era when a highly valued individual had facilitated a support group successfully for a number of years but following his departure several attempts to reinstate one had failed. I found myself wondering if I too might find myself in the hall of fame carrying the legacy of failure.

WHERE I WAS COMING FROM

There were a number of positive reasons (I rationalised) why I decided to respond positively to this overture. I had some slack in my diary and had agreed that an afternoon be set aside as a project slot. I wanted to maintain my competence in facilitating support structures for professional staff since a three-year supervision commitment had recently ended. I was impressed by the student's commitment, motivation and passion in wishing to effect positive changes in her work environment through her post-registration studies. The student had already demonstrated motivation and competence by undertaking a questionnaire eliciting the views of her colleagues within the multi-disciplinary team regarding the need for a support group. The results of this questionnaire indicated a strong level of support for such a development. The student had already spoken to her line and unit manager obtaining tacit support and consent to seek out an appropriate facilitator.

SETTING UP SHOP

I proposed and agreed a time limited three-phase programme of six weekly meetings in each phase to be held in the afternoon. This was a total of 18 meetings over a six-month period. I wrote to the unit manager indicating my willingness to facilitate the programme subject to the usual contractual arrangements between the trust and the university. I received written permission to proceed. Before the start of the programme, I arranged an introductory meeting with the ward team to discuss aims, objectives and ground rules. For my own benefit, I decided to make process recordings of each meeting immediately after the event using an audio dictaphone system. My approach to facilitation was informed by a number of considerations. My educational practice and consultancy is informed by a social systems/psychodynamic orientation. My intention was to create space to allow issues to emerge spontaneously through free association. No attempt would be made at the interpretation of silences which would be allowed to descend and persist on the principle that they were necessary for reflection on feelings and for the incubation of ideas. Where appropriate I would maintain a light touch but would make helpful interventions to prompt further reflection rather than leave the group high and dry or dug in and stuck.

During the introductory discussion there was an expectation that the group, if successful, might continue beyond its prescribed life. We discussed the possibility that I might use my recorded material at a later date as the basis for an article for publication and permission was given with the proviso that I ensured anonymity. The ground rules agreed covered commitment to attend, punctuality, confidentiality; respect for opposing points of view and responsibility for self-disclosure. To enable the nursing staff on the ward to be released, an approach was made to the manager of the intensive care ward requesting assistance with staff cover. He agreed to this and my impression was that people were generally being helpful and supportive.

PHASE ONE

Background

After the success of the initial day for rapport building, I turned up on the first day of the formal programme. As I had by now oriented myself to the unit, I went straight to the dining area where the meetings would be held. I re-arranged the area, set the chairs in a circle and waited expectantly. After 45 minutes of sitting by myself experiencing a mixture of feelings ranging from perplexity, awkwardness, anger and frustration, a member of staff came in to apologise. There had been a crisis on the ward and we agreed that we would close the meeting. This was an inauspicious start to the journey.

During phase one, attendance over five meetings ranged from four to seven people with an average attendance of five. Apologies that were received for each subsequent group meeting, ranged from one to four with an average of one. Although this represented a core group of attendees, the membership shifted considerably from one meeting to the next across all three phases. All attendees were female.

The second group meeting: taking off

A great deal of relief was expressed that the support group had finally taken off (as they saw it). Two members discussed their experience of working with difficult clients and attention focused around feeling unsupported by colleagues since there was nowhere to take feelings evoked from such encounters. One client example related to the surprise and disappointment felt by one member who despite making strenuous efforts to be available to discuss issues with her, was verbally abused by her and to make matters worse, found herself feeling betrayed when she later discovered that other members of the team would not work with the client for exactly that reason. They had not forewarned her.

Several examples were presented by members illustrating how they had no choice but to carry highly emotionally-charged feelings home and one particular member described how she had been left high and dry and on one occasion, on returning home, had spent the evening in tears on the telephone talking to an off-duty colleague. There was a claustrophobic sense of being hemmed in by the system with no space to think. Hope was expressed that the space afforded by the support group might help them deal with some of these feelings although there was also concern that the group itself was vulnerable.

Commentary

There was a heightened expectation that the group would provide staff with the space to ventilate and contain their feelings, incubate ideas and think through some of these powerfully emotive experiences. I sensed that the space afforded by the group might well assist with the development of strategies for moving beyond the experience so that the insights generated could be taken into the wider staff group for discussion and if useful, refined, formalised and utilised in the development of policy and practice. There was a strong feeling that the burden of emotional labour was carried by a few members of staff and a more equitable system was needed. There was also a concern that staff be allocated and matched with clients on the basis of compatibility. Members felt vulnerable and fragile and I gained the impression that most believed participation in this enterprise was an act of faith. I sensed that there was much ambivalence since members openly expressed doubts as to whether or not they could trust their colleagues. Allied to this, there were issues around group members' ability to hold each other within the group and uncertainties were expressed about their colleagues' willingness and ability to hold the fort so they could attend. Despite the optimistic expectation that the group was taking off, I felt that they were merely at the checking in stage, or, as one member had put it – 'here to see if we can still talk to each other'.

The third group meeting: feeling unsafe

An atmosphere of tension and paranoia surrounded this meeting. The discussion started with a member of the group announcing how upset she was because a colleague had announced he had been made redundant. This triggered enormous anxiety within the group, some of whom were on short-term contracts. Concern was expressed about the way the issue had been managed and anger was directed towards managers who were perceived to be authoritarian, clumsy and insensitive. Concern was expressed about one member in particular (not present) who was felt to be vulnerable and ways of helping were explored. This then developed into a second attack on the uncaring managers who were perceived to be too preoccupied with their targets and a number of examples were given to support the view that people were being sacrificed in the drive for economic efficiency.

Commentary

There appeared to have been little consultation around the events and people felt vulnerable. I felt there were parallels with last week's discussion relating to how systems can lock people in leaving them with little conscious control over events. Here was a situation that landed on their doorstep from another part of the system. The group had to make space in their meeting to express their feelings and make sense of it as in the case of the member in the previous meeting who felt compelled to spend hours on the phone talking through emotionally-charged feelings relating to ward events in her own time and at her own expense.

The fourth group meeting: the rescue attempt

There seemed to be more energy at this meeting and indeed the group seemed very pleased with itself. As a result of last week's discussion, management had been approached by the senior member of the group with a proposal to which they (management) agreed. This agreement provided a lifeline (three months contract) to the members of staff who had been made redundant. An absent member at risk of losing her children as the result of a custody battle became the focus of discussion. This resonated with a number of members' personal circumstances. There was an acknowledgement of her special needs and the burden this placed on the team but in particular, two members in whom she confided. The group acknowledged how hard it was for professionals to seek help and the discussion moved on to centre on the perceived difference between men and women in their openness and willingness to disclose. There was conscious acknowledgement for the first time that the support group membership was constituted solely of females but that the men were playing their part in holding the fort.

Commentary

I commented on how flattering it must be to be the 'chosen ones', to be perceived to be available and able to contain others' feelings of distress. On the other hand, how difficult it must be for the person seeking help, knowing that they posed a burden. I had an image of the person concerned bobbing up and down on the ocean trying to drop anchor in both calm and stormy weather, encircling an island which was close by but never daring to go close enough to take advantage of the island as an anchorage point. This, I relayed to the group to illustrate the difference between sharing within a subgroup as opposed to sharing the issues with the group as a whole. I felt it was easier for the group at this stage to explore personal issues through the case of the absent member with whom they identified. They were keeping things at a safe distance but getting closer to the heart of the matter in their own time and on their own terms.

The fifth group meeting: big brother

One member opened the discussion by disclosing that she had received a telephone call from a senior manager asking her to log in the diary the time at which a particular member came and went off duty. She initially did this in good faith and then checked herself as she realised the significance of what she was doing. There was a chorus of support around the room as she declared that she had great misgivings about what she was being asked to do as this was a management strategy designed to keep check on someone already involved in a disciplinary dispute. There was widespread support for her position of non-compliance as the group did not wish the team to be involved in a surveillance exercise on behalf of management. There was on the other hand, acceptance that the member of staff concerned was unreliable and irritation was expressed by some members about her lateness and lack of availability to patients. The discussion then moved on from feeling irritated to feeling good and special as there had been much praise for the nursing staff from patients regarding the amount of time spent with them. This led on to a discussion around the pressure to increase beds, the prospect of nurse-managed beds and its impact on staff time. One member pointed out that there was an external audit coming up and hope was expressed that through this, the clients' voice would be heard and the nursing contribution would be recognized.

Commentary

Clearly members had initially been put on the spot without realising it. This led to a preoccupation with their feelings of anger and irritability towards management and then with how good it felt to be special. The irritability factor crept in towards the end as people talked about their concern at the disproportionate distribution of specialness towards some people and not others. This evoked a feeling of paranoia regarding the forthcoming external audit and questions were raised about what the clients might say about them. This resonated with the earlier theme of surveillance.

The sixth group meeting: feeling controlled

There were feelings expressed regarding how two new members of staff on the ward might be feeling and although these concerns led to a discussion as to whether they might be invited to the support group, no consensus was achieved. There was a general feeling of uncertainty within the group and acknowledgement as to how unsafe things were. This discussion centred on how little control staff had over important areas such as budget holding and decision-making. Fear was expressed as to the prospect of further redundancies particularly for those on short-term contracts and around the imminent imposition of identification badges for all staff. There was some idealisation of the group regarding how useful it had been.

Commentary

Members were feeling vulnerable and unsettled. The two new staff on the ward who had been rescued by the team were supernumerary. No one in the team quite knew what this meant in practice and attempts to clarify the situation had failed as the person who had made the decision was on annual leave. This left the staff team feeling ill at ease, disempowered and somewhat impotent in the face of not knowing quite how to help them feel at home, fit in and make a contribution to the work of the team. A paranoid sense of being controlled by powerful external forces pervaded the meeting. I felt relieved to be having a two-week break.

PHASE TWO

Background

The first meeting was cancelled due to staff shortage and the second and third meetings went unrecorded as I had found it difficult to open myself up, concentrate and attend to the processes during these two quite intense meetings. This coincided with pressures in my personal and work life around this time. I found myself at the end of these particular meetings rushing back to my work base feeling overloaded, emotionally numb and almost intellectually paralysed such that I could not bring myself to collect my thoughts and commit them to record. I rationalised that I would return to the task later on. This, I never did. On reflection, there was so much going on at the time that I did not have the mental capacity to fully open myself up to the experience of the group in order to process and make sense of it.

I note however, that I made the following entry in my recorded notes, 'The group seemed to mirror what was happening outside in the wider system – there was a high level of distress, sickness and absenteeism. People were not in place at the right time, the group seemed fragmented and members preoccupied with team conflicts and the impact of current organisational changes'. I reasoned some time afterwards that my intellectual paralysis mirrored the difficulty which the group itself may have felt in containing and making sense of the powerful forces which were reined against it. Only the fourth and fifth meetings were recorded. The sixth meeting was cancelled by agreement in advance as the majority of the regular group members were on annual leave. I felt relieved by this cancellation and welcomed the space. The attendance ranged from four to six members, two apologies were received.

The fourth group meeting: inter-professional conflict

One member opened the meeting by saying how glad she was to be there and a second member endorsed this. The first member talked about her difficulty in getting doctors to discharge their responsibilities and undertake the work that needed to be done. It appeared that a nurse had admitted a client in crisis and the doctors refused to acknowledge, support and service her decision. Members expressed anger at this and felt that the nursing role was undervalued. Anger was directed at a consultant who was concerned with who had signed a medicine form while ignoring and avoiding the obvious distress of one of his clients whom he steadfastly refused to see. In addition, the fragile equilibrium of the ward had been disturbed by the presence of the police involved in an admission and by the prolonged presence of independent auditors conducting interviews of staff and clients. These external agents caused a great deal of disruption (and paranoia). As a result, two clients became so disturbed they had to be transferred to the intensive care ward.

Commentary

The conflicts and tensions in this meeting related to issues around power, authority and the ineffective re-negotiation of professional boundaries. The nursing staff felt impotent and powerless to direct resources to where they were needed most. This lack of control was accentuated by the presence of unfamiliar people entering the system creating additional stress leading to high levels of anxiety among staff and high levels of disturbance among the clients. I noted that the cause of the disturbance was neither acknowledged nor dealt with since the most disturbed clients (who were there for care) were projected out into another part of the system.

The fifth group meeting: the knot

This meeting was interrupted throughout by a disturbed client who soon became the focus of discussion. On each occasion she had to be physically escorted from the room by a group member. Throughout the meeting there were a number of additional distractions as the members found themselves 15 minutes into the session competing for attention with piano and vocal music emanating from a music therapy session on the floor above and half an hour later, a lawnmower outside started up when the groundsmen returned from lunch. At the beginning of the group one member spoke about having a knot in her stomach and expressed her disappointment that she had only managed to give 15 minutes to a client during the shift. The rest of the discussion centered on the disturbed client and the group's feelings of frustration directed towards her, articulated by one member as 'hitting one's head against a brick wall'. There was a general consensus that trying to understand her was like trying to unravel a knot.

Commentary

This was a group (and facilitator) struggling to maintain a sense of coherence in face of invasive interruptions from outside. The preoccupation with staff interactions and the disruptive client illustrated a continuing theme concerned with the relationships between staff, the division of labour and the delivery of care. I made some reference to the need to acknowledge staff with differing attributes who might take different approaches to the same client. I felt a sense of impotence and was relieved that this phase had come to an end. On reflection, I felt the meetings had left me feeling depleted of energy and I felt concern for the group members carrying such intense pressures in their everyday work. I was beginning to appreciate how difficult it was to maintain a degree of emotional resilience and therapeutic optimism from day to day.

PHASE THREE

Background

The first meeting of phase three was cancelled due to staff shortage. When I arrived for the second meeting I was approached by one of the regular group members who seemed alarmed. She had unsuccessfully tried to contact me by phone during the morning. She informed me that the group wanted my permission to extend the support group to the other members of the multi-disciplinary team as there had been a crisis. I took a deep breath and instinctively suggested we discuss it at the end of the group and if there was a consensus, the multi-disciplinary team members could be invited to the following week's meeting. The group agreed and at the end of the group, the decision was taken to invite the multi-disciplinary team to the next meeting. The invitation was extended but was overruled by the unit manager who intervened unilaterally after deciding it was not appropriate. As a result, this meeting did not take place, the following two meetings were cancelled due to staff sickness but the sixth and final meeting was held. Attendance at the second and last meeting held at four members per group and apologies ranged from two to four.

The second group meeting: the secret

There was a short silence at the beginning and the group felt tense. When the discussion eventually opened up, members shared their feelings about recent ward events. There was talk about interviews, interrogations and visible management presence. There seemed to be a struggle going on in the group to contain and hold back something – a secret perhaps? It finally emerged that one of the senior members of the staff group had been suspended and an inquiry established to investigate allegations made against her. Another member of the group had been informed that her contract had not been renewed. There was a pervasive feeling of low morale, insecurity and paranoia since other members of the group were also on short-term contracts awaiting confirmation of renewal. The discussion then centred on the benefits of the previous meetings in so far as people were more aware of the emotional burden one member had been carrying in relation to a particular client. Subsequently, a more egalitarian distribution of effort emerged as the other team members seemed more willing to step in and take the strain. There was a great deal of reference throughout the discussion regarding the perceived benefits of the group and it was noted that members of the wider multi-disciplinary group had commented on how calm and contained those who attended the group appeared to be. They acknowledged that this may have been a reason why the others had sought entry. We discussed the request by the multi-disciplinary team and it was agreed that one member of the group would extend an open invitation and distribute the ground rules.

Commentary

This was a difficult and tense meeting. The suspension issue did not come up directly within the group, it surfaced towards the end. This had been a major blow to staff morale as the individual was a respected senior member of the support group. In addition, they were understandably feeling anxious, threatened, uncared for and some members were anxiously awaiting renewal of their short-term contracts. It seemed very much like a system under enormous pressure and felt unsafe. The group seemed to be coping with their sense of paranoia and despair by taking flight periodically into idealising the group and instilling the hope that it would make things better.

The sixth group meeting: spring cleaning

Due to the cancellation of the previous two meetings, I rang in the morning to check that staff would be able to attend and received confirmation that the meeting would be held. One person turned up on time and three members came in ten minutes later. The discussion opened with members talking about their feelings regarding the current situation. Some felt safe, others less so. Two members were now on permanent contracts but others were not and some had left in unsatisfactory circumstances. The discussion then deteriorated into long drawn out complaints about smoking and areas where smoking took place. Anger was expressed at having to see clients in interview rooms that had been left reeking of smoke. This led to the suggestion that perhaps ionisers should be ordered to help with the problem. The discussion then centred on the need to change, to develop new practices and anxieties about having a new line manager. Anxiety was expressed about the democratic credentials of their new manager and there was much discussion about how undemocratic and out of control things had become. There was a recognition that fragmentation of communication had occurred within the nursing team as members took flight into subgroups for protection. A strong sense of despair and heightened anxiety about the future was expressed. The discussion optimistically see-sawed around acknowledgement of the need to adjust and adapt to the changing circumstances tempered by a recognition of members' anxiety at the prospect of change. At the end of the group there was a prolonged period of silence that was finally broken by one member who said how much she had valued the group and thanked me for facilitating it.

Commentary

The reference to the ioniser made me think that the group wish was to get rid of the impurities or toxins from the system. This made sense since the re-structuring and reorganisation in light of the recent incident suggested that management were 'spring cleaning', and, closer to home, group members had been spring cleaning emotionally within the group. I had a mental image of the group as a lightweight boat without a rudder bobbing up and down, going round in circles on a stormy sea. This was a difficult ending as there had been many losses along the way. There was sadness surrounding the loss of familiar structures and ways of working; the loss of their respected line manager; the impending loss of the support group and the dream (that it would make things better) which it may well have represented. There was considerable anxiety about the presence of a new parent who represented current and future hope. I thanked them for their contributions and tried to positively reframe what seemed a bleak ending, pointing out that from this experience new shoots might grow and new developments take place. On saying goodbye and leaving the room I felt a heavy feeling of sadness tinged with a light sense of relief that this journey for me at least had ended. On reflection, I found myself (I think) relegated to the pantheon of heroic failures residing in a place somewhere in the collective mythology of the team should they choose to remember.

ON REFLECTION

On failing to thrive

There is a complex relationship between our internal world and the external environment with which we interact. Which is most decisive in determining outcomes, individual agency or the context in which we play out our lives, is a recurring focus of debate. In the mental health field, staff are confronted with this question on a daily basis. In this case, did the support group fail to continue beyond its prescribed life because staff were ambivalent or defensive and so unconsciously left it to wither on the vine towards the end? Did it fail because of the pressures exerted by the system that on occasions blew it apart or were the seeds of destruction already built in when it was set up on the back of a student project with a naive tutor agreeing to facilitate it on a time-limited basis? Perhaps it was a combination of all three? Should we even talk in terms of failure since it clearly was valued by the group members.

Pressures in the system

Perhaps this is how it is for many nursing teams in mental health inpatient settings that by their very nature face the daily challenge of containing and managing emotional disturbance and its collateral fall out. In this case, the group space had been grafted on to a highly pressurised socio-emotional system thus providing a safety valve for the small group of nursing staff who elected to attend. The pressures on the ward team that flowed through this socio-emotional decontamination chamber were often so powerful and difficult to contain that on occasions the group evaporated behind a screen of sickness and absenteeism. Only 11 out of 18 (60 per cent) of the planned meetings took place. When the meetings did take place, they mirrored accurately the pressures within the team and at times became a turbulent socio-emotional space where staff vulnerability, client pathology, managerial and interprofessional power politics converged to create a toxic vortex.

Power and authority

Understandably, staff felt they had little control as the system appeared to have developed a dynamic of its own leaving them feeling hemmed in, powerless and with little space for reflection or critical thought. Power and authority seemed to reside in places far removed from the ward where most of the clinical work and interactions with clients was conducted. The ward manager held the budget but a senior manager made the decisions when and how it would be spent; the bed occupancy figures compiled by the ward manager for collation were returned in a form that could not be understood having been massaged to comply with trust targets. The carefully considered decision by the group to extend their meeting to the wider multi-disciplinary team was over ruled by the unit manager. Corporate trust financial insecurity represented by the need to balance the budget translated into existential anxiety and personal angst as a number of staff found their position within the organisation severed and for some, their continuing existence under threat. This impacted on other colleagues who contained the emotional fall-out as best they could from within a fragile support network.

External forces

External agents also had a disruptive impact on the ward's fragile socio-emotional eco system. The presence of the police and the audit group raised the anxiety levels of the staff and escalated the degree of disturbance among the most disturbed and vulnerable clients requiring them to be removed to a safer place. The audit group in particular, initially welcomed and perceived as potential allies by the nurses in their struggle for recognition by the doctors, turned into interrogators and persecutors.

Boundary management

I feel my decision to let the group make the decision to extend an invitation to the multi-disciplinary team to attend was an error. I should have realised that, given the circumstances, a separate crisis meeting was more appropriate. On reflection it would have been better had I kept the helm, said no, and preserved my authority and the integrity and boundaries of the group. My concern to portray a democratic persona to the group may well have played a part in this unfortunate decision as did the pace of events. As a result, the boundaries shifted and it was left to the unit manager to put the brakes on. I had by default placed her in the position where she had no choice but to exercise her authority and re-draw the boundaries for the group.

A nomadic space

The location of the group and its boundaries within the system was significant. The meeting was held weekly in the dining area but I had overlooked the implications of this at the time when, at face value, I accepted it as the only suitable space available in which to convene the group. This was a public area that had to be cleared of both people and utensils after lunch; where furniture had to be moved around and chairs re-arranged in a circle to create space for the meeting and then replaced afterwards. Significantly, this was a temporary space that closed after the group. This perfectly mirrored the status of the group within the system, temporary, short lived, and on the periphery (a visiting guest on the premises). This should have alerted me to the ephemeral status of the group since it did not warrant the provision of a more appropriate, dedicated group room within the unit.

A safe space

It is essential in this type of work to have a safe space where the facilitator can explore the issues with the help of a supervisor. Unfortunately I was slow in seeking to set up such support where I could take my feelings and reflections. When I did, I failed to secure funding as this form of activity was deemed to be outside the remit of my organisation's business plan. As the programme progressed, it became more and more difficult to set up an informal arrangement as work pressures built up around me and I took my eyes off the proverbial ball. This was unfortunate as it is exactly for these reasons that supervision for the facilitator is essential and had I secured such an arrangement I might have been more alert to, and pro-actively responsive to some of the emerging dynamics which left me feeling vulnerable and at times overwhelmed.

Sustainability

Realistically, group support meetings cannot be grafted onto systems, they must emerge and develop organically from within a culture of reflexivity to ensure their legitimate continuation and preservation. In this case, the support group members and the wider nursing team were inordinately emotionally intelligent individuals struggling to make sense of a system that had been set up to care but which frequently seemed to entangle staff and clients in an enterprise which often led to very different outcomes. They coped admirably with their own personal issues and were at pains to ensure these did not overly compromise their relationships with clients. Such commitment and talent however, cannot thrive in isolation and needs to be embedded within a wider organisational culture whose sympathetic structures possess sufficient emotional intelligence to support a good-enough environment for the promotion of reflexive practice.

A challenge for the future

Although the rhetoric of clinical governance is ever present, everywhere, we have failed to significantly prioritise quality enhancement (as opposed to quality control) through the provision of individual supervision and support groups for nursing staff. Unfortunately to date, these spaces have not been seen to be worthy of investment as legitimate and integral elements of clinical governance structures. Although there are excellent examples of reflexive practice within some areas of mainstream mental health service provision, they are the exception rather than the norm and often occur by default rather than by design. They represent a small oasis in an otherwise barren desert of widespread neglect. If we fail to make the case to convert the cosy rhetoric of clinical governance into meaningful action over the next decade, history may well repeat itself and we will find that the cobbler's children will continue to be the least well shod.

ACKNOWLEDGEMENTS

The nursing team on 'Maypole' Ward for sharing their space. David Kennard for prompting me to write. Liam Clarke and Gail Salsbury for their helpful comments on the text.

Chapter 10

Authority and control – working with staff groups in children's homes

Michael Maher

EDITORS' INTRODUCTION

Part I of the book makes several references to the influence of the organisation in which the staff support group is set. Michael Maher's chapter goes further by illustrating how behaviour is a product of the organisation, and his approach to working with it. He writes about establishing staff support groups for different teams in a single organisation, and offers an understanding of how a strategic decision to offer staff support groups is affected by the organisational dynamics. His aim for staff support groups to 'make more aspects of the work open to authentic discourse' echoes the aim stated in Chapter 1 'to enable staff to use the full range of their emotional responses in the service of the task'. Maher introduces the systemic model, which gives the reader another way of conceptualising and working with group process. He is clear that working towards this aim can take years, as does the deeper aim of cultural change. Interestingly, his finding that half of staff benefited from support groups is consistent with our conclusion in Chapter 8 from the research evidence on staff support groups in general.

This chapter will describe work undertaken with a group of children's homes in a local authority setting in southern England, over a period of ten years. The goal of the staff groups was to help develop the functioning of the teams, to increase their capacity to contain the impulsivity and self-destructive capacities of the children they worked with. It will describe how I approached this task, what happened along the way, and how I developed my own approach, moving in search of what would work best in this context, from a group-analytic to a systemic model.

THE CONTEXT

First, some history and a description of the context. I was employed to work with the managers and teams of eight children's homes. I was taken on at the same time as the operational manager of the residential service, and paid on the same grade, as an internal consultant. My job was added to over time and became more diffuse in its focus, but this was the core of the work from the beginning. The reason for this unusual appointment had been prompted by some severe difficulties in the residential service, which had been through some upheavals immediately prior to my arrival. I arrived into a context where some of the homes were functioning well but others were in a state of freefall, with mass absenteeism from the staff who were supposed to work there, many staff having left or about to leave, others staying but reserving the right to be angry, blaming and complaining. Inevitably, given the prevailing conditions that were applying, the children and young people placed in these unstable homes were largely out of control. They were scared and in turmoil at the disintegration of the 'places of safety' they had been sent to as refuges from the places of danger they had lived in previously. As they acted out their understandable fear and anger so the dangers around them increased, leading to a familiar vicious spiral, which needed to be arrested.

None of the above is unusual. Running a children's home is always an experience of living on an edge; a successful home is one which creates a culture where these anxieties are contained most of the time, and where crises and outbursts are things which can be survived and learned from together; it does not take much for that line to be crossed, and it is hard to recover when a culture of containment is lost.

The primary need in an unstable context such as this is not consultation, it is management, and this was provided well by the residential service manager, backed up strongly by a committed head of children's service, and supported by me. Over a period of time actions were taken which stabilised the service, allowing a more settled picture to develop, of homes beginning to function in a more containing and task-oriented manner. The task of consultancy shifted from crisis management to development – the system could now begin to shift from survival to development, with an aim to achieve transformation, at least in parts.

I had some particular qualifications to take on this task. I had been deputy director at Peper Harow, a therapeutic community for adolescents, and had subsequently managed a group of children's homes in an inner London borough. I knew about these children from hard won, first hand experience. I had also trained in group analysis, a clinical approach to working with people in groups that has applications to organisations; it combines psychoanalytic theory with an understanding of humans as essentially social animals.

In group analysis psychotherapy is 'by the group, of the group, including the conductor' (Foulkes 1975) and paradoxically, to the conductor, the group as a whole and its therapeutic functioning are as important as the individuals.

(Brown 2006: 93)

I wanted to offer what I had learned from both sets of experiences to the managers and staff engaged in the draining, infuriating, frustrating, fascinating and occasionally rewarding task that I, by now, knew a lot about.

Two of the homes worked with children with a range of disabilities, including clients who could be unpredictable and difficult to manage; the other seven worked with non-disabled clients who presented significant challenges – they were often distressed and often angry. They were frequently aggressive and violent, oppositional, volatile, desperate for attention, rejecting of attention when it was given, had low self-esteem and were insufferably arrogant, claimed autonomy and independence and had deep dependency needs, had the ordinary wish to explore, test out, try things out for the first time and impulses which were perverse and dangerous. They at times wished to harm others, and harm themselves. They had been harmed themselves – by physical and sexual abuse, by neglect – often by adults they loved and needed to trust in. Most of them had multiple tries at living in substitute families before they came to the children's homes, so had the secondary trauma of failed attempts at attachment overlaid on the loss of their primary attachments. They were ordinary children and extraordinary – normal and special.

In other words we had a population within which there were a significant number of developing personality disorders – particularly borderline and antisocial. And that's all I want to say about psychopathology. The task of a children's home is to contain all of the above and do more than survive it, and my task was to help create the conditions with the teams which made that possible.

THE GOAL AND MY APPROACH

The success of the role would be measured by increases in the homes' capacity to contain and work effectively with high occupancy levels of groups of the types of children described above. Success would be measured on multiple fronts – good inspection reports, reduced use of the private sector and secure accommodation, the views of the children themselves, the views of referring social workers, notions of 'best value' and so on, so the success of the consultancy was inextricable from the success of the overall management of the service.

My approach to all nine homes was to engage with them to try to build cultures of enquiry (Main 1990). This concept derives from the world of therapeutic communities and relates to the building of a system where behaviour is approached as having meaning, which, if explored together, can develop a collective understanding. It is important to emphasise here that it is the act of struggling to explore, to make enquiry in the right sense of the act, which is important. A misuse of the endeavour would result in competitive interpretation that would keep all the pathology in the children and keep the adults free of it, creating a distance and a disavowal which would be counter-therapeutic and anti-task. Culture of enquiry also relates to another central tenet of therapeutic community work, where a disturbance in one part of the system – member of staff or resident – is necessarily related to what is happening in the system overall. This approach depends on everyone involved being able to find and engage with their natural curiosity about themselves, each other and the group as a whole.

With this in mind I negotiated with the managers of the homes – some of who were new in post – offering them regular consultation for themselves and fortnightly groups – of an hour's duration to begin with – for the teams. The goal of the groups was to deepen the range of communication available, to make more aspects of the work open to authentic discourse. From the start these offers were related to differently by the different managers. Some seized on the offer and wanted more; others were more wary. On exploring what was contained in the wariness, I discovered a reluctance to disturb the functioning of teams which were perceived as working well – they had high occupancy, managed incidents effectively, and had low staff turnover. The attitude was summed up in the view – 'If it ain't broke, don't fix it.'

This response presented a dilemma in terms of authority and control and fulfilling the goals of my job. This was to help develop the residential culture and I wanted to approach this by deepening and widening what it was possible to talk about in the teams, to increase reflective functioning and, importantly, to increase thereby the safety of the contexts. This was in the belief that impulses (which are bound to be there because of the nature of the provocation in the work), when admitted to and explored together in the company of colleagues, are less likely to be acted out than those which are just kept in, taken personally and suppressed. At the same time I knew that no intervention would succeed without the wholehearted active support and involvement of the manager (both the manager of the service and the managers of the homes) and the wariness was understandable. Over time these homes and I settled on a compromise – I attended staff meetings, offered training interventions, related to the teams in a number of ways but did not have regular sessions with the purpose of building a culture of enquiry via exploring in depth the impact of the work on the group, and the group on the work.

At the time, and in retrospect, this was an unsatisfactory compromise. It meant that I had a less close relationship with some of the homes. This varied over the years, as I was closer or further away, in response to how the homes and I managed this essentially unstable and ambivalent arrangement. I will return later to the system issue of which this was symptomatic.

I established regular fortnightly sessions with four of the homes. None of them had had such groups before. With each of them the groups started as internal case discussions, concentrating on an individual child each time, with a view to exploring what that child 'held' for the group. I used the frame of the question 'How does this child make you feel?' as a way of introducing group work norms to staff who had not hitherto encountered this way of working. This addressed a number of issues. First, it established that it was not 'unprofessional' to have 'negative' feelings in relation to a resident, and no one would be subject to disciplinary action if they admitted to them. Second, it began to teach the group that such reactions could be information about the child's experience, and what was being re-created in the current relationship. Third, it normalised and legitimised the fact that there would be differences in the group, and to hold a difference in feelings in relation to a child was information which, if not taken just personally, could be something to be curious about, to explore in the service of building a culture of enquiry. This case study approach was an embarkation point for establishing a culture where the staff groups became established. It was always my intention to move from this structure to one where the primary focus moved from the child or the group of children to the adults and the group as a whole. Over time, most of the groups made this transition, from talking about the children to talking about themselves, and the discourse shifted in focus from 'How does this child make me feel?' to 'What is it in me that is mobilised by how this child relates to me?' This transition shifted the gaze from out of the group, focusing on the child's psychopathology, to within the self and among the group, exploring things that the staff group had real knowledge of and influence over in the here and now.

After five years of sustained work with the staff groups there were changes to the structures: I took on a wider remit, developing a unit which took on working with nine residential special schools as well as the children's homes (which had increased in number by now to nine also). I employed a range of staff in this unit, including two in the role of consultants to work across the schools and homes. At this point I handed over the groups to them, and they developed them in line with their own expertise and what the staff groups wanted from them. I supervised them as conductors of these groups, and kept in touch with their development from a distance. After three years of this one of the consultants retired, and I stepped back into running three groups for about a year, before I too moved on.

CHANGES IN INTERVENTION STYLE FROM EARLY TO LATER GROUPS

The narrative so far has concentrated on the context and the goal, and how I approached the early groups; the next section will focus on a shift in the theory base I used and what happened in later groups.

The change in my approach from the early work with the groups to my later involvement reflected two main developments. First, the groups had developed, and had several years of regular sessions in which to develop their capacity to engage in a mature and reflective way. Second, I had become increasingly interested in and influenced by the approach to working with groups pioneered by Yvonne Agazarian, under the title of Systems-Centered Therapy. This approach offered approaches to organisational development that gave significant advantages, particularly in relation to clarity about what the goals of the groups were, and how to make interventions as conductor to help the group move towards its goal. This approach particularly helped me understand that the central issue in the work with the children, and in the staff groups, and in the system as a whole, was that of the authority issue. In the 'Theory of Living Human Systems' developed and articulated by Agazarian, how a group relates to authority dominates the early phases of development, and is a task for all groups and individuals to explore, recognize and find their way through, over and over again.

> The dynamics of the authority issue are the fulcrum dynamics of the process of change in all human systems, from simple to complex. Taking issue with authority occurs within the self, in dyads, in subgroups, in small groups, in large groups, and in the system as a whole. It is common to individuals, families, social and business organisations, communities, and nations. It is as old as the human race and it fuels revolutions and wars. It never sleeps; a leviathan, it stirs restlessly in the depth of human experience and is easily aroused.
>
> (Agazarian 1997: 241)

The authority issue exists as a set of pulls in all of us. In a work context, it can be expressed as a pair of intersecting axes.

- Axis one: I want my manager to inhabit his/her authority fully, to really demand of me and push me, to be clear, direct, authoritative, rigorous, to recognize my potential and work me hard to draw it out. And I fear that my manager might do this, and hate the prospect of such pushing and pressure with a deep and powerful passion.
- Axis two: I want to own and inhabit my own authority fully, to know what I know, to be 'my own man', to do what I know to be the right thing, despite the consequences, and to live with the full consequences of not shying away from this. And I fear and dread the overwhelming sense of responsibility that comes with inhabiting such a state of being, and shrink from it.

This issue is then converted, in the early flight and fight phases of group development, and in individuals within systems, into relations with authority that are enacted as compliance (flight) and defiance (fight), while certain roles are created and maintained in order to contain the projections that accompany these positions.

In order for a group to achieve communication and work it must have sufficiently explored the pulls briefly outlined above, and the intense feelings that go with them. In systemic practice this is done through teaching the group to subgroup around similarities, rather than relating over differences, and exploring feelings and thoughts rather than explaining them or acting them out, with the therapist active in ensuring that flight defences are undone and fight energy is directed towards the therapist and not between group members.

The context I was working in was not a therapy group, it was a work setting. At the same time, the authority issue in a children's home has the potential to be utterly virulent. The children all had powerful traumatised versions of issues with authority that they brought with them, inevitably, into the work. Their reactions to the inevitable frustrations of having to share the world with other people who insisted on behaving in ways they did not want mirrored in an exaggerated way the ordinary frustrations of the staff group who carried their own versions of this universal experience. The roles they adopted in order to manage these painful encounters with the far-from-ideal had their origins long before, as had the roles adopted by the staff tasked with helping them. This had the potential to be repeated throughout the system, as staff behaved in ways the managers did not like, and the home as a whole behaved in ways the children's department did not like, all of which were necessary and healthy at times, but would produce frustrations which could undermine the successful functioning of the home, if not addressed successfully.

With this framework in mind I returned to work with the staff groups to help them explore the authority issue, learning to differentiate the roles that they were being induced into by the powerful suction the children's behaviours exerted on them as a group. I taught the staff to do this through subgrouping, by bringing in an experience in the here and now, in relation to an aspect of the work, and asking if anyone else had a similar feeling or thought or physical sensation that they could add, to build on what had already been said. Different reactions were held back until the subgroup had explored its experience, and then another subgroup could explore their experience, and find if others had similarities they could bring to build on each other's work. I worked on the premise that if the authority issue could be explored, it could provide a base from which intimacy and work with the children could be reliably and authentically achieved.

In approaching the groups in this way, I found it helpful to work with the group to differentiate some fundamental things – between anxiety and reality, and between thoughts and feelings in particular. Although there are many defences that staff in such contexts need the skills to recognize and undo, moving from negative predictions (which produce anxieties based on thoughts) to the present reality (of not knowing what the future held) was particularly critical. Anxiety is a dominant force in a children's home working with a challenging group, and in order to work in the reality of the here and now the group had to learn how to undo the grip of anxiety enough to be present and have access to their curiosity, thereby making the culture of enquiry possible again. Similarly, in a context where one of the primary goals is helping the children learn how to contain their feelings, and not fear them and act them out, it was also critical for the staff to be able to do this. We spent a lot of time working on the capacity to discriminate between thoughts and feelings, so that we had a base from which we knew what the differences were, and what came from where. An example here may be useful.

Example

A group, which had some recently arrived staff in it as well as experienced staff, were preoccupied with the recent loss of a long-established resident, who had moved on to a long-term foster family after several years of intense work. They slipped into talking about him and anxieties about the suitability of the new family. I reminded them that the task of the group was to focus on us, and perhaps the feelings in us which were activated by this loss. This was enough to move the subgroup who were speaking into dealing with personal feelings relating to endings and loss, and the roles they went into as ways of managing these painful experiences. I reinforced this by interrupting when speakers used 'you' when they meant 'I'. This provoked some irritation with me, which I encouraged them to explore, but the subgroup chose to continue the work on exploring the experience of loss, relating it to their own experience of the boy and what resonated in this experience with their own experiences of other losses.

Quite quickly a number of people in the subgroup were in touch with strong feelings, some to the point of tears. It was clear that there were strong feelings of love mobilised in the moment, and this seemed authentic, both about the experience of a relationship of several years and also about personal experiences triggered by this event, with work in the subgroup about the similarities in this loss to other losses, and important differences. I reflected to myself that some years ago, when I started work with this group, this level of feeling would have been seen as 'unprofessional', and now it was not. In fact, not only was it allowed; it was seen as key to the task of helping them inhabit a place from which they could help each other and the children manage their experiences of loss.

At the same time another group of staff were silent. I asked the silent subgroup what their experience was, and one of them replied that he felt awkward because he did not feel the losses that the other subgroup felt. He felt a bit envious of them. I asked him what he wanted to explore, the feeling of envy or the feelings he had about the boy that were different. He said he wanted to explore the feelings about the boy, which were of not liking him, and finding him 'too much', and being relieved that he had moved on. I asked if anyone else felt similar feelings, and there were, and that subgroup (which included the new staff) explored those feelings together. This subgroup developed, with some work about the sense of energy which was available when they were in touch with the feelings of anger at the abuse they had suffered at his hands.

The first subgroup listened to the second subgroup work together on how they related to their own experiences, and there were recognitions of this aspect of the reality. Later in the session, the manager brought in information relating to a new admission to the home, and a discussion developed about the timing of this and what needed to be done by way of preparation.

Systems survive, develop and transform through the discrimination and integration of difference. In this example we had a group that had the capacity, in that moment, to allow for differences in experience, and for these not to be experienced as an attack. Critically, the work of exploring similarities and integrating differences was done, which allowed for the task of the home to be pursued without it being sabotaged. There are many common pitfalls in the scenario illustrated above – the context might not allow for feelings of loss to be acknowledged, and judge such reactions to be 'unprofessional', in the belief that good childcare should be based on neutral transactions in which adults hold back from working too closely with children (not getting overinvolved). In a context where feelings are allowed, the myth can arise where only 'positive' feelings can be admitted to, and 'negative' ones must be suppressed and disavowed. In a context where different feelings can be acknowledged, then the pitfall is for staff to separate around their differences; for the subgroup who are in touch with loss to react with hostility to the subgroup in touch with relief, relating to the difference as an attack on them and on their feelings about the child who has gone. In a group that has a pull to staying in exploring intimacy and avoiding work, there can be a loss of the goal of the group, which in this case also involved making plans for the arrival of the next resident.

The work I describe above made it possible for differences to be accepted. This helped differentiate between the past and the present, and helped group members recognize habitual roles used for accommodating themselves to aspects of reality that are experienced as painful or unwanted.

This linked the group to the group of children they work with, avoiding the projection of pathology from the adults into the children, and helping them recognize the roles they adopt in similarly difficult environments. This allowed the group to separate the leaving of the one child and the arrival of the other, thereby avoiding the team relating to the new child in terms of her difference from the old child, and helping them be open and curious in how they approached welcoming the new arrival into the home. This group's work was built on the base of the analytic approach the groups had undertaken over some years, but we had shifted our focus and method. Different things became possible as a result, and the shift from them to us – and away from interpretation and into exploration particularly – emphasised the similarities between the adults and the children, rather than emphasising the differences. In this context, this was a culture of enquiry authentically at work.

THE WIDER SYSTEM DYNAMIC

I have already mentioned that this type of work did not take root in all the homes in which I consulted, and that there was a degree of compromise arrived at by way of my involvement and influence with the other homes. The key roles that made the difference between those that made full use of the groups and those that did not were the residential managers. Those who had an orientation towards therapeutic work with children, and those who were curious about where the group work might take them, made themselves available to engage with, and this provided the platform for the hard work involved in establishing the group culture and the culture of enquiry in these teams. The attitude of wary ambivalence in the other groups was shared by the operational manager of the service, and although we worked closely together to bridge this split the default position – of not needing to fix something that wasn't broken – was always there as a restraining force in trying to spread the culture throughout the service as a whole. There was something I did not do, early in the story of these years, which I can now see would have given us a way of addressing this basic fault. (I use this phrase as a nod towards Balint (1968) rather than as a specific reference to his book of the same name.)

The residential managers met monthly with the operational manager and myself. The operational manager chaired the meeting, and it concentrated on business. It was an unsatisfactory meeting, in the way that many business meetings are chronically unsatisfactory, in that over time a number of managers expressed to me their feelings of unease in the experience, which they related to feelings of rivalry and envy, or fear of envious attack. I asked if it would be possible to bring this experience into the meetings when they were at play, but none of them felt able to take this step. The meetings were experienced by me as avoidant and unproductive, yet I seemed strangely paralysed and unable to influence them into being more what I wanted them to be, which was very different from the confidence with which I inhabited my role in the children's homes. Rather than use this experience as information and be curious about it, and see if anyone else was curious about it too, I took it just personally, and went into a role which I now can see was avoidant, defending against the reality of legitimate differences between the operational manager and myself.

What I could have done is try to model something in this group with the residential managers about attention to process and capacity to model a culture of enquiry. I could have started by introducing a feeling of dissatisfaction with myself, and ask if anyone else shared in this, and see if the group could begin to explore its experience in a way which members could have access to a fuller range of their resources and could remain curious and open – in this case about how we as a group stopped ourselves from having the kind of group we wanted to have. Perhaps I could have asked for a structure where this could have been explored with the operational manager and myself before bringing it to the group, and this might have been possible in a joint supervision. Without managing to model this, to bring the important experience of scepticism into this group, a split was maintained along a fault line between my role and that of the operational manager and the potential for taking the culture of exploring together in groups deeper and wider across the homes was as a result compromised.

This does not invalidate the work that was achieved across the service as a whole, but it does explain why the approach I espoused was taken up with such degrees of difference across the homes. For a staff support group to succeed in this context, everyone involved would need to be clear about what the goal of the group was, and so what success would mean. In my mind the goal of the groups was to support change – cultural change at depth, which would assist the groups' and the homes' move from survival to development and transformation. This goal was shared by the managers and then the staff of the groups that joined in the endeavour. Perhaps those groups, tacitly supported by the operational manager, which did not engage at that depth did not share the same goal – at a time of bombardment from central government and the parent organisation, of massive increases in demand in regulation and bureaucracy, with all the frustrations inherent in that process, it is not surprising that their priorities might be elsewhere.

In the often-repeated mantra about not fixing that which is not broken, we have a clue – an important goal in the system as a whole related to not changing, and this goal was in competition with the goal I was working for, that of adaptive change. Staff support groups in a system where the goal is 'no change' will only support staff to stay the same, and will become essentially redundant. To prioritise the goal of survival over that of development can be an entirely appropriate managerial decision; the task then is for those in the system to keep their boundaries open enough to recognize when the shift from survival and no change to development and change is possible and necessary, and engage in pursuit of the new goal. In the meantime, habits become established and roles become locked, and this can be difficult to perceive and harder to change.

My own belated recognition of how sclerotic some of these relationships had become led to my decision to move on from the organisation. I had confidence in the groups I had been conducting that they would be able to continue to maintain the cultures of enquiry we had worked on to establish together. They would develop ways of keeping this culture alive that would be different from how they did it with me, and this was a positive and necessary condition of maturity – that they could inhabit their own authority in relation to this task, and insist that it was given the importance it warranted. With the rest of the system I came to the conclusion that someone else might have a better chance of success to undo some of the role locks we had created between us, and so open up the resources in those groups whose boundaries had become rather closed to my inputs.

CONCLUSION

What can be generalised from this experience? The experience of success was based on paying attention to the context, being clear about the goal of the group and the role of consultancy in relation to the group moving towards the goal. The consultancy helped the group establish a culture of enquiry, and helped them have access to their natural curiosity in negotiating the authority issue, which it needed to repeat time and again, becoming more adept in undoing the defences that kept them in flight, fight and role locks with authority and each other. The experience of where the consultancy was less successful related to failure to pay sufficient attention to the wider context where the service operated, where the system did not offer a clear enough goal – there were competing goals at play, and noise in the system in the shape of ambiguity, contradictions and redundancy.

Nevertheless, the service as a whole performed at a remarkably high level over these years, and success was indicated on every measure. The service ran with high occupancy levels; staff turnover was low; children reported satisfaction with the circumstances in which they lived; the outcomes relating to education and health all showed significant improvements. Children who would have been lost were held. The homes felt like good places to be.

The staff groups played their part in this success, helping staff explore important areas of experience in the service of the task. When this was aligned to the ethos of the home (as embodied by the managers), they had the potential to develop and transform how adults related to each other and the children in their care, having a huge impact on what it felt like to work and live there, thereby making a transformative impact on the long-term outcomes for the damaged and vulnerable children who lived there, and for whom the system exists.

Chapter 11

The insider as facilitator: conducting a group for hospital clinical team leaders

Chris Powell

EDITORS' INTRODUCTION

Many staff support group facilitators work as clinicians or managers in the same organisation as the group they are facilitating. In some ways this may seem an easy solution to some of the questions and negotiations that need to be addressed in setting up a staff support group, which we take the reader through in Chapter 4. However, this situation also creates a number of issues that do not confront the external facilitator. In this chapter Chris Powell addresses these and describes how he understands and works with them in his own organisation. These include complex decisions around confidentiality and the sharing or withholding of information across hierarchical and personal boundaries. Powell here extends the discussion of boundaries in Chapters 5 and 6. As most of the examples in Part I of the book involve an external facilitator, this chapter gives a valuable alternative perspective.

Many staff support groups employ external conductors or facilitators. However, this chapter addresses my situation in facilitating a support group in the organisation in which I work. This will be illustrated by some of the dilemmas this presents. The group concerned supports a new tier of clinical management in a psychiatric hospital, comprising seven nurses promoted to clinical team leader positions. The intention is to support them in a demanding role, to facilitate collaborative working between them, and to encourage a management style consistent with the values of the organisation, a Quaker based independent charity. As well as being the facilitator of this group I am also head of the organisation's outpatient service, a psychotherapist with a background in organisational consultancy. In the context of this chapter my theoretical approach is to apply the principles and understandings of group analysis to organisational settings, paying particular attention to the network of communication within staff groups.

THE BACKGROUND TO THE GROUP

The Retreat is a psychiatric hospital with 112 beds, founded by a Quaker tea merchant, William Tuke, in 1796 as a radical and pioneering alternative to the orthodox practices of the time (Glover 1985; Borthwick *et al.* 2001). Unusual at its foundation, it is still unusual today, being one of only two not-for-profit, independent psychiatric hospitals in the UK. Its governors are still drawn from The Religious Society of Friends (Quakers), and the NHS funds 90 per cent of the people receiving inpatient services. So it is neither NHS nor a private sector hospital, but rather, a genuinely charitable institution.

The Retreat's organisational and managerial structure evolves and re-evolves over time. In 2004 it became clear that the three clinical service managers who managed the inpatient services were becoming over-stretched. Senior managers were taking a more strategic role and clinical service managers' roles had developed from directly running their units to taking on more responsibilities on behalf of the organisation, such as developing clinical governance, liasing with NHS commissioners and other purchasers and improving staffing structures. It was clear they needed to focus on organisational roles, but also that each of the inpatient units needed clinical leadership closely involved in its running.

This coincided with a period when senior managers had become aware of stresses and difficulties in some relationships between staff and managers. Senior managers decided to appoint clinical team leaders to manage the everyday running of the clinical units, reporting directly to the clinical service manager for their service. These clinical team leaders were identified from existing staff on each unit, some of whom were already adopting leadership or managerial roles. It was clear they needed training and development in these roles, but senior managers were also aware that other sorts of support might be necessary. The chief executive invited me to facilitate a staff support group for the clinical team leaders, with the intention of supporting their adoption of these roles. The underlying assumption seemed to be that such a group could be effective in helping them to manage the stresses and difficulties of the job and to help them be effective in a critical managerial level of the organisation.

These assumptions seemed consistent with the benefits I believe differing kinds of staff groups can bring: work discussion groups provide a place for dealing with the emotions inherent in mental health work (Ho 2007); staff sensitivity groups enhance relationships and promote co-ordinated and cohesive working (Haigh 2000); work groups provide a way of inspecting and understanding dynamics in the wider organisation (Whitaker 1992); and staff consultation groups can allow participants to develop the ability to look outwards to the wider context as well as inwards towards their own work (Rifkind 1995).

In autumn of 2004 the seven clinical team leaders were asked to set up a monthly meeting to organise the rotas for various staffing requirements, such as site co-ordination and staff rotas, and also to allow opportunity for them to attend a support group meeting. They organised this efficiently and liased with me to identify a suitable time. I suggested we meet in my office in The Tuke Centre, which is separate from the main Retreat building, hoping this would increase the sense of stepping aside from their work and limit potential interruptions. They had identified a need to meet for two hours, the first hour to organise staffing, the second for the support group. I offered to attend both parts of this meeting to gain an understanding of how they were working together and what their role involves, as well as to facilitate the support group.

This format ran successfully for several months and I began to gather some insight into the pressures and demands of their jobs. The director of clinical services then proposed that clinical team leaders have a whole day each month to meet for training, support and liaison. This was accepted and the staff support group was incorporated into this day, with me now joining just for the support group time, which we extended to 90 minutes. The group has continued to meet monthly since then, with some changes in membership as individual clinical team leaders have left the role or organisation, and others have joined.

MY ANTICIPATORY CONCERNS

From the start I was aware that my role in this group was different to a facilitator entering from outside the organisation. All the members of the group knew me; my own work as a manager was visible to them. Their managers were my peers and colleagues in the organisation. I was identified with the senior management of the organisation having been selected by the chief executive for the job and sitting on a number of organisational bodies in which they did not participate.

However, I was also aware of differences, which I hoped might provide some degree of distance and external perspective. They were all nurses, and although I am a psychotherapist my background is not in health care. I was unaware of many of the standard processes and cultures of their work, so they would have to instruct me. I do not work in the main hospital building, so am insulated from some of the gossip and intrigue inherent in any organisation. I am used to working in the structured, time-boundaried ways of a centre for psychotherapy, which is very different from the more fluid structures of inpatient units. I am a man, while six of the seven original members of the group were women.

So I entered the group with a series of dilemmas in mind. I wondered whether it would be possible to be neutral as internal facilitator and who, if anyone, would set the group's agenda. I was unsure how helpful or otherwise inside knowledge of the organisation would be to me as the facilitator. Would it enhance my understanding, or simply hinder an enquiring stance, and 'evenly suspended attention, not making premature judgements' (Armstrong 1995: 41)? I also wondered whether I would experience conflicts of interest in the wider organisation on issues about which I might have confidential information. I was also unsure about the expectations of the group as there was much less time spent in negotiation of a contract to provide this group. How much would I be expected to facilitate support between peers in the group, and how much to mentor as an experienced manager?

Perhaps my deepest uncertainty though was whether it would be possible to ensure the group provided containment for the pressures of working in an organisation when I also experienced pressures from the same organisation.

THE EARLY LIFE OF THE GROUP

In the first meeting of the group, we discussed and agreed the aims for the group.

1   To discuss work and professional issues safely and confidentially.
2   To offer each other support and advice.
3   To share how you are tackling issues and learn from them.
4   To identify issues or problems of common concern and decide how they can be tackled.
5   To support each other in raising concerns with managers.

This fifth aim emerged from two sources. Internally to the group there seemed to be a sense of being separate from The Retreat's senior management, and a fear of not being listened to when concerns were raised. External to the group, I was clear that the request to establish the group emerged from an organisational context where senior managers wanted staff in general, and clinical team leaders particularly, to act more independently and take more authority. I believed the ability to negotiate effectively for change with senior managers would be central to this, and that clinical team leaders had more power than they realised, but which could be more effectively applied if they worked collectively.

In the first few meetings of the group the following themes emerged.

• They were uncertain about the scope and responsibility of the role and some of its aspects. This included whether they should remain part of the nursing numbers or be supernumerary, freeing them from nursing tasks for their managerial responsibilities, and also their responsibilities for the main reception desk while acting as site co-ordinator for the hospital. The role of site co-ordinator was particularly anxiety provoking, as it involved acting as the main point of contact and co-ordination for any unusual or untoward incident happening within the hospital. This also included ensuring that any incoming phone calls are dealt with if there is no one else available outside normal working hours. This was experienced as very demanding alongside being responsible for the clinical unit in which they work.

- They perceived that to tackle administrative tasks they would need to leave the ward area and its immediate nursing demands, but some group members did not have access to a separate office and others who did found it very difficult to use it.
- There was concern about equality between them, particularly the share each took for organisational roles such as acting as site co-ordinator. There were also concerns about inequality in salary levels between staff in different clinical units.
- There were common concerns about staffing issues, especially in relation to the use of bank and agency staff. There was a common wish for someone to co-ordinate staffing issues rather than dealing with them individually.
- They frequently felt important organisational information was not reaching them or that they were not consulted on issues affecting them.
- There was a common perception that there were insufficient opportunities for meetings and support from line managers.

A number of these themes have persisted and thrown up dilemmas for me.

DILEMMAS OUTSIDE THE GROUP

Participation in organisational meetings with decisions affecting group members

After a few meetings of the support group I found myself in an organisational meeting where an issue was raised relating to cover of the main reception desk outside office hours. This was an issue that clinical team leaders had discussed at length on account of the impact these arrangements had on them, particularly when undertaking the role of site co-ordinator for the hospital. What was proposed in the meeting seemed to be contrary to what clinical team leaders wanted and would not address their difficulties. I felt myself in both a difficult and powerful situation. It seemed difficult to be party to a decision that I knew to be inadequate, and yet I only knew this because of my privileged knowledge from the support group. I also felt the difficulty that the decision of the meeting was proposed and supported by my colleagues who were the clinical team leaders' line managers and yet who seemed either unaware of, or to have a very different understanding of their concerns. I felt a desire to protect the clinical team leaders. I also felt powerless to share information from confidential group sessions. I was also aware of an erroneous feeling of power and perhaps even superiority, that somehow I knew better than my colleagues, and that if I was to display my knowledge they would have to defer to it. In short, I was drawn to feel I was better positioned to make this decision than my colleagues, including those who actually managed these services and had long and first hand experience of inpatient work and management.

Eventually I decided to speak, contributing in the form of a question, wondering whether the meeting knew what impact this decision might have on the site co-ordinators (mainly clinical team leaders). The first response was that we did know, but I pressed that it was worth consulting with them before implementing the decision. That was agreed. What I was unable to tell at the time, and still do not know, was whether others lent my opinion additional weight by knowing I now had this particular relationship with the clinical team leaders and so might have inside knowledge.

On reflection, I noticed I was identifying with the clinical team leaders, and feeling some separation from senior managers and clinical service managers, my actual peers. It was tempting to feel they did not really understand the clinical team leaders, whereas I did. It seems I was beginning to gain access to some of the pressures and feelings experienced by the clinical team leaders, and this included a sense of their managers not properly understanding or supporting them. I was aware this could also be at the expense of the wider organisational perspective available to senior managers. The particular issue under discussion had not been major, but I was gaining a sense of how a preoccupation with particular individual unit's or individuals' needs could become distorting. This in turn led me to wonder about the difficulty of my colleagues' roles in trying to attend to the needs of individual units and their clinical team leaders, while simultaneously taking account of wider organisational needs.

Engaging in peer support with the managers of group members

At the same time this group began, my peers and I were offered the opportunity to meet in our own facilitated support group. This I welcomed and joined. However, from the outset I was aware of trying to sit and talk with colleagues, on whom some of the people they line managed had been passing comment, sometimes negatively. They too were aware of this situation. This was not the only issue of conflicting managerial boundaries in the group: the facilitator of the group, a consultant clinical psychologist, worked in services managed by one of the group members for instance.

From the outset there was some acknowledgement of these boundary issues, but they remained in my mind as an underlying tension in the group. Eventually a point was reached where a colleague considered withdrawing from the group, I believe at least partly because of this tension. However, with encouragement from the group this person remained and with some further acknowledgement of the issue, tension seemed to lessen and greater mutual trust and disclosure seemed possible. My discomfort was mirrored, however, in meeting with the clinical team leaders and I return to this below.

Responses to senior managers asking about members of the group and their concerns

About a year into running the group a senior manager approached me about the clinical team leaders. Part of the enquiry seemed straightforward, asking how well the group was working and how best to provide other support and development for clinical team leaders. However, I again found myself uncertain how much to say, having formed views about aspects of the organisational management structure that seemed to exacerbate difficulties for clinical team leaders. I acknowledged this uncertainty. With the joyfully clear vision of hindsight, I now see the opportunity presented to propose more direct communication between that senior manager and clinical team leaders. This could have been facilitated by me or someone else, given that clinical team leaders often found themselves struggling to communicate clearly either individually or as a group with senior managers.

Instead, I was caught with a sense of the impossibility of straightforward direct communication as a means to effect change. The alternatives being to breach confidentiality to some degree, or else to remain silent on issues about which I had strong feelings. I now believe my feelings and inability to see a potential solution were closely connected. It was because of my direct involvement in the organisation and my personal investment in its success that it felt as if it really mattered to see things addressed. However, it was also my involvement in the organisation that made me more than usually prey to the dynamics that were impeding straightforward communication.

In working with work groups as a consultant or facilitator, I am aware of having to deal with the expectations placed on me to provide a solution or to do something that the group or individual need to do for themselves – Lawrence's 'politics of salvation' (Lawrence 1994). It is the boundaries of the group – such as starting and finishing when agreed, and operating within agreed terms of engagement – that allow me to sit back, reflect on these expectations, and then offer them back to the group in a way which allows it to deal with the problem for itself (Rifkind 1995). However, I was not alert to the fact that with this group, I was operating in relation to it, without the protection of group boundaries, by virtue of being in daily contact with people in or related to the group in some way. I was discovering that although Clarke Kent's mild mannered dress might contain the steely body of Superman while going about his daily business, I was vulnerable to being caught off guard while working in the same environment as the group to which I attempted to offer impartial facilitation.

David Armstrong describes the need for consultants to inspect and work at the organisation within themselves, and that without this it is too easy to become contaminated with the organisational equivalence of counter-transference (Armstrong 1991: 40). I was discovering this danger increases exponentially while working as a consultant within an organisation of which I am part.

DILEMMAS WITHIN THE GROUP

Having access to different or more accurate information than group members

Early on I realised that group members were discussing information that I understood differently from meetings I attended and they did not. In one particular instance they discussed a decision taken at a meeting at which I was present. Their view of this decision was very negative, but it seemed to me that the reasons for the decision had either not been communicated to them or had not been understood. Also, that they were misconstruing the decision. The dilemma was whether I would correct their understanding, or allow them to continue with a discussion and feelings based on what I believed to be erroneous information. It did not seem helpful to me they should feel and act as though they were being badly treated when I did not believe this was the case. However, I was also reluctant to reinforce an idea of me as being the expert in the group who could provide information and answers that would make everything right. As I thought about this I could not see any way to deny my part in the organisation and so eventually fed in my perspective on this particular issue. I was surprised to find first that I was not readily believed, and then that the information provided was being discounted as an exception that only served to prove a rule. I found myself being drawn into defending the position of their managers, and hurriedly retreated by steering the conversation to another area.

Later, in another session, faced with a similar situation, I think it was considerably more useful that I reflected on the idea I was being drawn into, that there was privileged information somewhere outside the group, and that if only they had access to it everything would be fine. This is a recurrent fantasy within organisations, the idea that things are going on higher in the hierarchy which are kept secret. Of course sometimes this is true, sometimes not. However, the fascinating issue is that when access to that information is given, of itself this does not seem to make things better.

What is harder to look at is the reality of being in a subordinate position and the anxiety this can provoke. I reflected something of this to the group, that perhaps they imagined that if there was better communication from senior managers things would work better. However, perhaps senior managers might have similar feelings, that it could be hard to communicate with clinical team leaders and that team leaders kept things secret from senior managers. As they began to think about this, the problem became one that they could own and do something about by making sure they had more regular meetings with their managers, and trying to raise clearly things they were finding difficult.

Hearing colleagues criticised in the group

This is the parallel to the dilemma identified above, where I found myself present as members of the group spoke negatively of my peers and colleagues.

The dilemma here was whether to respond at all, to defend my colleagues, to collude with the attack, or whether to be able to do something else. Over time in the group it became clear that the clinical team leaders had a tendency to be hard on themselves, being very conscientious, committed to their jobs and loyal to the organisation. They would be quick to see problems as a result of some failing in themselves. However, some of them could also at times be quick to feel neglected or ill treated by the organisation or their managers. Listening to their accounts of their experience it was clear that some things were particular to an individual, others were common. Where the difficulty was with an individual the group was effective in providing support and helping the individual think about how they might deal with it. However, when the experience was shared in some way, the tendency was to ascribe blame externally including to their line or senior managers. I believed it was important the group did not feel it was compromising me by talking about these things as it was necessary to create the proper room to explore negative feelings and experiences. This is a normal feature of staff support groups I facilitate in other organisations. Nevertheless, it left me feeling uncomfortable.

I have attempted to resolve this for myself with a similar mechanism that I use with people who are reluctant to be negative about friends or family in psychotherapy. People are often reluctant to speak badly of their parents or partners, but I explain I know they are not really talking about their actual husband, mother or whoever. I explain that the person they are describing is only their idea of that person. I do not know if it is an objectively accurate picture of what that person is like in real life. So I keep in mind that they are describing an idea of someone, that is actually part of themselves. This, for me, is a much harder trick to pull off when hearing about someone I actually do know. However, I have discovered that as time goes on I have been able to maintain the idea that the manager being described in the group is at some level a fantasy of the group, and in fact an entirely different person from the one I know. All that is being described is a relationship, and as such it finds itself mirrored in the relationships that emerge within the group, between the members and between the members and me. This in turn helps me to reflect on my part and therefore the group's part in whatever the difficulty being described might be.

OTHER DILEMMAS

The role I hold in relation to this group continues to throw up a variety of dilemmas. Attendance at the group tends to be consistent with most people there most of the time. However, sometimes individuals or even the whole group find it difficult to attend. I have come to understand that they don't attend because they feel deprived in some way – of time, status, appreciation, resources – but end up starving themselves of something that would nourish and support them. I believe that they have internalised the sense that they are there to be exploited, that their needs come second, third or even last, when put alongside the needs of patients, the organisation, staff, colleagues, or even families. However it is painful to face this and the group activates that feeling, as they have to sit and listen to others, while they feel themselves to be at breaking point. I wonder whether they can explore this properly in my presence, if I am identified with the management structure of the organisation they feel to be putting them in this position. They must wonder, as I do, how I will handle it if an individual's needs are at odds with the organisation for which I work; if for instance, the organisation seems for its success to need them to work harder, whereas they need for their survival to work less.

In fact I do find that I have a different sense of responsibility to this organisation than when working with people from other organisations. This is despite being clear that I have a direct responsibility to the other organisation, not just to the individual I am working with, if the organisation is funding or commissioning the work I am doing.

I believe I reconcile these dilemmas by coming to understand them as false dichotomies. I believe there is usually no real exclusive conflict between the needs of the organisation and those of the individuals working in it. Crudely put, this means that healthy or prosperous individuals create and are part of healthy, prosperous organisations. When such conflicts actually do exist they are best dealt with straightforwardly. There needs to be acknowledgement, acceptance and resolution, no matter how painful.

With this in mind, I think I also have come to see myself as only ever imagining myself to be separate to the external organisations to which I consult. Systems theory suggests that once we enter an organisation as external consultants we become part of its system and so begin to change it by just being there (Rance 1989). Although the dilemmas are not as acute as those I face in working internally to my organisation, they often exist in similar or equivalent ways. I am potentially caught between the agenda of the person or department that has commissioned the work, and that of the team with which I am working, for instance.

OUTCOMES SO FAR AND AFTERTHOUGHTS

This group continues to meet, and I think, flourish. Over its three years, a number of clinical team leaders have left their jobs, some for natural reasons such as retirement, others because the job is genuinely difficult and demanding. However, as a group I see them as having developed in confidence and effectiveness, and this has coincided with and been a factor in changes in the organisation, which seem to me to have improved communication and devolved more power and decision-making to individual teams.

There have been a couple of points when the group and its usefulness have been informally reviewed, notably when there has been a change in senior management. On both these occasions group members have been vociferous in wanting to defend this group for their professional support and individual well-being. However, there has been a lack of clearly agreed criteria for evaluating the group. This is something I would routinely do with other groups and wonder whether my closeness to the organisation has hindered me from being as rigorous as I might in other settings.

I can see how both my commonality with and also separation from the members of the group stood to have an impact on the core skills I use in facilitating any group for learning, development or support. I have core tasks I attend to as facilitator of a staff support group. Of these, maintaining the structural and emotional boundaries of the group is critical, in order to build a secure, trustworthy environment for sharing of experience and challenge. I knew this was challenged from the start of this group. I have wondered whether boundaries could have been set up better. On reflection, I think probably not. I have experienced some puzzled responses when trying to negotiate things within the organisation in the ways that I would as an external consultant. It is as though when hiring a plumber we might expect to give clear details about the nature of the problem, arrange a time to do the job, and agree an appropriate price. However, if you are a family member unlucky enough to be handy with a spanner, you might have to make do with being told to 'fix the tap' and then endure hostile shouts when you turn the water off only to discover someone is trying to run a bath.

I am often inclined to think about the 'what if' in relation to my work as an organisational consultant, and have to remember to be content with doing an adequate job in the circumstances. I have had to discover and remember in this case how much easier it is to maintain these boundaries within the confines of the group, than in the everyday interactions of the organisation. In taking on and maintaining this role I believe there is a small bit of me that has to be held back from the organisation and my interactions with colleagues in order for me to maintain both my integrity and my ability to think and facilitate. I have made my organisational 'home' perhaps a little less like 'home'. This, of course is a natural consequence of a privileged position, one that I enjoy, and one through which I can make a significant and fulfilling contribution. A small, if real price to pay.

SOME PROS AND CONS OF HAVING AN INSIDER FACILITATE A STAFF SUPPORT GROUP

It seems to me there are some real pluses about working from this position. The insider may have a more detailed understanding of the organisation and the issues facing it. Using an insider also promotes the idea of the organisation as a body capable of promoting its own learning and change. This also means there is the possibility of learning being increased within the organisation, provided carefully negotiated boundaries allow for the appropriate sharing or dissemination of information. There is the additional advantage that using an insider avoids any potential difficulties of organisational or commercial confidentiality.

However, there are significant pitfalls. An insider may not push as hard for clarification as an outsider, depriving group members of the opportunity of some critical thinking. There will certainly be a dilemma if the facilitator has access to information not available to group members. It may be helpful to agree a ground rule for this with the group, clarifying what will be done when this occurs. My own experience lends itself to noting to the group when I think something may be otherwise to the belief of the group, but leaving the group to decide whether to pursue that further itself. I have also found it may be harder to remember to maintain the same disciplines as when working as an 'outsider', such as establishing clear processes for review and evaluation. Without doubt it is less comfortable having to live with some of these disciplines every day in your organisational home, than being able to walk away from them in an external organisation.

I am glad I took on this role. I have learned a great deal from it, much of which was about things that are very much less evident when working as an outsider. I am also clear that the group members and the organisation have benefited. Any potential internal facilitator would be advised neither to leap too quickly in to such a role, nor be too hasty to refuse the opportunity out of hand given the potential hazards and gains.

Chapter 12

Managing personal and professional boundaries

Ewa Wojciechowska

EDITORS' INTRODUCTION

In Part I the management of boundaries is discussed in the context of the role of the facilitator (Chapter 5) and dealing with common problems (Chapter 6). In this chapter Ewa Wojciechowska explores this core aspect of the group and the facilitator's role in greater depth, with examples of how personal experiences or needs can have major impacts on people in their work situation. She also illustrates an important aspect of boundary management – when it may be appropriate for the facilitator to see a group member on her own. This chapter takes us squarely into the realm of feelings, echoing one of the defining functions of a staff support group identified in Chapter 1: to enable staff to express, discuss and manage difficult or painful emotional responses. Central to this is how the facilitator pays attention to and uses her own feelings. Linked to this, Wojciechowska develops further the discussion in Chapter 2 about personal motivation in members of the caring professions, and the need to balance the tension between our idealism and realism.

INTRODUCTION

Vignette – an erotic fantasy
A young teacher in a special school sat sobbing in a team meeting. Colleagues tried to console her, but were at a loss to know what was inspiring the tears. Eventually, she was able to tell that, the previous night, she had had an explicitly erotic dream (about one of the older boys). She was deeply ashamed about this and – in her mind – had come in to apologise and to say goodbye, since she was sure the team would wish to have nothing to do with her.

It came as quite a surprise to hear from colleagues that her conclusion was quite wrong, that this was not seen as a resigning matter. It was pointed out to her that her dream/fantasy was to be understood (certainly not to be acted upon), but that her openness, her self-knowledge and her ethical awareness were all characteristics that marked out her suitability for this work. It was suggested she discuss this with the staff support group facilitator (and between individual guidance and exploration in appropriate team settings including the staff support group, the young teacher flourished).

Comment

There are occasional situations when it is helpful for a group member to see the staff support group facilitator individually. For example, as in the vignette, if there is a highly personal and potentially embarrassing issue. Others may include when difficult interpersonal situations would benefit from discussion, but an individual needs help to think how to raise it in the group. In general if seeing someone individually, it is helpful to discuss how best to take the material into the staff support group. The vignette provides an example of how a personal matter can erupt into the workplace. Fortunately, this did not frighten her colleagues: there was enough wisdom and experience available to her for the matter to be thought through, rather than reacted against. Had that not been the case, a promising career would have been ended prematurely and wrongly. It is usually very difficult for people to discuss sexual ideas in groups. However, this young woman immediately understood the importance of her dream being open to exploration and receiving support from her colleagues. Sometimes individual sessions are useful to help people to do that. This is an example of highly personal material being brought from an individual session to the group that helps everyone discuss difficult issues.

THE PERSONAL AND THE PROFESSIONAL

The premise of this chapter is that managing the boundary between the personal and the professional, and between individuals and the group, is crucial in determining the psychological well-being and success or failure of the health care professional in their work context.

There is an immediate potential conflict in the mental health field – it involves the donning of a professional mask that is meant to frame our conduct at work. However, there are always 'slings and arrows' to be borne like any place else and the advice is often heard – 'don't take it personally' – but, what do we mean by 'not taking it personally?' If we don't take it personally, how do we take it?

The 'personal' impinges on the 'professional' and vice versa, both in the present and the past. People often talk of 'taking (their) work home'. Less often does one hear of people 'taking home to work', but just as work may flow into non-work time and contexts, so it is vice versa.

A member of one of the staff support groups I facilitate said recently: 'I don't know if I'm bringing my real self or my professional self here (and what is the difference?)'.

One cannot work all day and every day with emotional disturbance and be unaffected by it. It can be disorienting, exhausting, frightening – or some combination of these – particularly when these resonate with one's own private anxieties, fears or concerns (especially when the latter occurs outside one's direct awareness). This is neither good nor bad, neither right nor wrong. It simply *is*. It can be managed well or managed badly, but it cannot be wished away. In some settings, dealing with more extreme pathology or with life and death issues, there is often an attempt to 'laugh' it away with a certain 'gallows humour'. Such humour has an important role to protect against what are perceived as socially unacceptable feelings, such as fear or aggression.

Alongside this sits another dynamic: a tendency towards idealism and idealisation. Most of us, especially at the beginning of our career, can identify some degree of notions of vocation or 'wanting to help'. Our attitudes have yet to be tempered by the reality of the situation, as they assuredly will be.

What follows seeks to cast some light on these countervailing dynamics:

- how the personal and the professional are constantly colliding;
- how our wishing for/imagining the best often denies the reality of the situation;
- how an understanding of the importance of boundaries will support and protect staff.

My role as facilitator is to hold onto and understand a maelstrom of unconscious and conscious feelings in the group, some of which are my own and some of which belong to group members. I have to process these both in and then outside the group and give back to the group my digested understanding of these feelings. This then allows them to work through and move on in their work. The other major part of the role is to create and maintain a safe and reflective space where members might feel free enough to talk openly to each other about their work and its impact on their boundaries. In order to maintain this space, I have to hold the boundaries of time and place, sometimes becoming quite fiercely protective! In one hospital where I work, the group before mine (meeting in the same room) has a tendency to run over time, I have to be quite assertive in letting them know they must respect our time limitations. The group analytic concept of 'dynamic administration' where the facilitator takes full responsibility for all aspects of the setting up and maintenance of the group is a cornerstone of successful facilitation (Barnes *et al.* 1999: 53–4).

WHAT DO WE MEAN BY BOUNDARIES?

If we start with the basic idea of a boundary being that which keeps some things in and other things out, such as human skin, we can infer that people need boundaries in order to maintain a separate identity and have a place from which to relate to another human being. For example, if a person gets physically too close to another without invitation, their personal space can be threatened. They may then react quickly and sharply by moving in the opposite direction or pushing the person away from them. This is because their personal space boundary around them has been intruded upon.

Thus it is seen how 'boundary' connotes a physical barrier. However, there are other more abstract and metaphorical meanings that signify a range of boundaries, invisible to the naked eye but nevertheless very real.

Molnos (1995: 27) speaks of four main categories when thinking about boundaries in therapeutic work: place, time, conduct required and relationships. We can safely transpose these to the area of staff facilitation as they have a similar important relevance.

- *Place:* constant, comfortable, clean, light, enough space.
- *Time:* regular, fixed, convenient.
- *Conduct required (of the facilitator):* regularity, punctuality, suspended action.
- *The facilitator's relationship with the group*: attitude, confidentiality, consistency, reliability, honesty yet no self-disclosure, abstinence.

These aspects identified by Molnos are very important but presented in this form rather static, implying something altogether more neat and tidy than is most people's experience. The day-to-day experience of staff is more fluid, more dynamic and rather messy. Where there is not a clearly defined boundary, it can be difficult to think; errors of judgement can be made.

Example
One night a senior male clinician in a mental health team found himself in the same pub as one of his (female) patients. Instead of manoeuvring himself away as discreetly as possible to another place, he found himself in conversation with her. She became upset, he held her in an embrace, perhaps to comfort her; and he then found himself facing allegations of assault with devastating

consequences for himself, his family and his team. Eventually he was cleared of the allegation and re-instated, albeit to another team.

What surprised me is that he seemed to be unaware of his professional boundary (perhaps because he was under the influence of alcohol which had impaired his judgement) and yet as a senior clinician he must have known about the perils of socialising with patients.

Within the personal boundary, we might think of one's hopes, fears, beliefs, attitudes and internalised experiences – in short, all the psycho-social components which make up the individual. The professional boundary, by contrast, refers to a defined task and role, within given values, behaviours and ethos – in short, a prescribed way of being for the carrying out of a particular role or task. For purposes of discussion, they are relatively easy to separate, as here. However, on the ground, day to day, they are much less easy to separate and can be the source of great confusion and/or discomfort for many staff and their teams. For example, the emotional loading that comes with this work is generated within the work, but it is experienced by the individual.

Where does the professional stop and the personal start?

What is being suggested here is that this overlap is often inevitable and has to be managed. That does not mean that overinvolvement with a client is inevitable but it is a constant possibility and the more this is held in mind and discussed the less likely it is to be acted out.

A staff support group needs a clear and firm set of boundaries that allows for an exploration of the personal–professional overlap. The maintenance of these boundaries provides a 'holding environment' (Winnicott 1971) which can be a safe and containing space in which to think (Bion 1961; James 1984). If the boundaries are transgressed, the container is fractured and insecure which can lead to a lack of trust in both the facilitator and the group.

WHEN A STAFF MEMBER REFUSES TO COME TO THE GROUP

Just as in a therapy situation with patients/clients, behaviour has meaning. Everything is a communication. Coming late, leaving early, bringing drinks in, leaving mobile phones switched on – these are all examples of issues manifesting themselves on or around the boundaries outlined above. They are all disguised communications to the group and are 'acting out' possibly unconscious feelings regarding the person's place in the team and/or in his/her life. (Acting out means communicating feelings in actions rather than words.)

The situation I want to talk about here is when a staff member refuses to attend the group. He is stepping outside the boundary altogether, but still communicating something by doing so.

Example

Martin (a highly valued nurse of longstanding in the team) had let it be known that he was not going to attend the group, one of the reasons being that I was not a nurse and therefore had no right facilitating a staff support group consisting largely, but not exclusively, of nurses. This was clearly a challenge to my authority in the group but also a communication about his feelings of powerlessness in response to both personal and professional issues.

I was interested in the role he played for the team – the silent and intransigent staff member who encapsulated the resistance of both staff and patients to change through dialogue and who was 'allowed' to miss the group in all sorts of creative ways. His refusal to join the group gave him a special place as the outsider – the one who wouldn't play the game, and this attracted anger and admiration in just about equal measures.

Sometimes it is necessary, for the well-being of the group, to hold individual one to one meetings to establish rapport and air concerns. I felt his unique position indicated it would be best for the group if I were to see him individually. I asked to meet with him on an individual basis. We discussed his fears and concerns about the group. It emerged that he had anxieties about exposing himself in the group, by becoming 'too emotional' or 'saying the wrong thing', potentially incurring humiliation and shame. He was also anxious about losing his job if he 'spoke out of turn' about his criticisms of the team leader. After this meeting he began to attend the group but only sporadically.

He continued to play a role for the nursing team, as described above. This was explored to some extent in the group but not resolved because of the continuing investment in it for both him and the team.

This is an example of working across a particular boundary in order to work better within it and is a reminder of how personal anxieties can be recast as professional concerns. The facilitator must be constantly alert to this and be in search of possible underlying meanings.

MOTIVATIONS FOR CARE-GIVING

Our motivations for undertaking this kind of work are varied and complex and frequently outside our conscious awareness, but it is likely that in seeking to care for others we are also to some degree seeking care for ourselves.

David Malan referred to the 'helping profession syndrome' in which the professional 'compulsively gives to others what he would like to have for him/her self, which . . . leads to a severe deficit in the emotional balance of payments' (Malan 1979: 139).

An obvious instance of conscious motivation, which is frequently seen, is where someone has a child with a severe disability (for example, on the autistic spectrum) and then goes on to make a career teaching/caring for/ treating children with the same or similar difficulties. Most people would think this unremarkable and quite understandable. But what is it that is being understood? Again, the motivations may be many and varied, but in all probability they include some measure of seeking a sense of 'agency', the desire to do something useful and purposeful in the face of the shock and impotence which may accompany parenting a very damaged child. This is an illustration of how personal grief, among other things, may be trans-formational, allowing the individual to use their experience constructively in the service of others.

There may also be unconscious motivation, as demonstrated in the following vignette.

Vignette: a patient commits suicide
Any suicide is distressing and emotionally arousing for those involved, whether personally or professionally. That is no less true when it occurs in the treatment situation. Nevertheless, in this illustration, Cathy (an experi-enced nurse) was unaccountably disabled in the aftermath of the suicide of a 16-year-old young man, an inpatient on Cathy's unit. In the immediate aftermath of his death, Cathy was a 'model' professional – liasing with the family, ensuring that all necessary recordings were made and supporting colleagues. She effortlessly adopted the caring role, which she maintained for a week or two, until she progressively succumbed to a persistent depressive state. Although she continued to turn up for work, it was apparent to colleagues that Cathy was not coping. Unfortunately, no one felt able to approach her about this.

Despite initial reluctance, she agreed to an individual session with the team's psychotherapist, which in turn led to a brief series of meetings. In the course of these sessions, she paid close attention to her compulsive need to care for others and it was soon clear that this was a longstanding pattern, first observable in her family of origin when she was driven to 'make things alright' when there was tension or conflict. In particular, it was essential to her to protect her mother from distress. In the course of all this, she recalled when her younger (then teenage) brother had tried (unsuccessfully) to hang himself. Despite the magnitude of this event, over the years it had become a buried memory. Along with this, she recalled that the suicide attempt had happened during her nurse training and shortly after it she had moved over to psychiatric nurse training – and until now she had not made that connection.

Although holding back most of the detail from the staff support group, Cathy was able in due course to share the 'headlines' with her colleagues, where to her surprise a number of people identified with her predicament and slowly began to share their own experiences. Within the group, this rich vein of material was important in deepening understanding and illuminating the interplay of personal and professional experience.

THE IDEALISTIC VERSUS THE REALISTIC

When people join the helping professions they often have idealising wishes to 'make things better'; to heal past hurts in their own lives through caring for others and to perhaps assuage guilty feelings about having harmed, in an imagined or real sense, their loved ones. One example of this is the worker who is driven to provide unsustainable levels of care. An unspoken agreement may descend on the team that these matters are not to be discussed, with the result that individuals are left burdened, alone, often in private misery. All of this is going on 'beneath the surface', as it were, whereas the surface appearance is commonly one of unquestioning goodness and idealisation of the care task.

Health professionals report increased levels of psychological stress, including anxiety, depression, drug and alcohol misuse and exhaustion (Tillett 2003). This no doubt arises partly from the pressures and demands of clinical work. But there is a wider concern that needs to be borne in mind, i.e. the complex relationship between the psychology of individuals, their own particular susceptibilities and vulnerabilities and their occupational choice.

Something of this kind is observed and discussed by many who facilitate staff support groups in health care teams, in both community and residential settings. Although all teams have their particularities, there are a number of factors which commonly present themselves. These include the following.

• Unresolved dependency needs, particularly in hierarchical institutions – notions of hostile dependence/'biting the hand that feeds'.

- Unboundaried and 'unprofessional' relationships between staff, and between staff and patients – especially dangerous when working with personality disordered adults. (See example of senior male clinician, pp. 150–1).
- Defences against 'madness' and chaos – exaggerating the madness of the patient rather than admitting to one's own anxieties and fears.
- Fear of shame and humiliation – collusion in the peer group, covering up bad practice.

According to Hinshelwood (2004: 36), 'job satisfaction is a fragile thing in mental health, and can be in short supply'. He argues 'If the staff could think about the way they are upset by their patients, they could learn a lot about the patients. The specific fears and anger the staff member feels point to specific fears and aggression in the patient – for instance, a burden of responsibility may derive from the patient's loss of self-control, which may need to be directly addressed. However, because staff cannot admit to these feelings – either to themselves or to each other – something of what they could know gets lost' (Hinshelwood 2004: 29).

Obviously, there are a number of factors that may be at play here such as a fear of precipitating disturbance in oneself, or indeed breakdown – or fear of how one might be perceived by colleagues or managers. There may be other factors too e.g. staff fantasies of omnipotence and/or overreliance on rational solutions (Hinshelwood 2004: 36). Then there are considerations of organisational culture. It is a commonplace to encounter denial of staff stress or managerialism that overly concerns itself with finance/administration at the expense of human relations.

Staff members often 'split off' or deny their own emotional needs for fear that they will be seen as a client or patient. Finding the right common language to express themselves within the group allows for the potential space to both think and feel, without fear of judgement, internal or external.

I see my role as helping them put their feelings into words by offering my own understanding of what the 'elephant in the room' might be or, put it another way, reading between the lines of their conversation and forming some conclusions about what is really being communicated beneath the surface.

As a facilitator, one can be both idealised and denigrated. Neither of these is real and they arise from imagined ideas and feelings about my capacity to transform the group's working environment or their own abilities. For instance, in one group, a nurse shouted at me 'you know nothing about what really goes on here! How can you possibly help me?' Then she flounced out, slamming the door as she went!

I often think of Winnicott's (1949) paper 'Hate in the Countertransference' in a situation like this (reprinted, Winnicott 1992). He talked about how the mother needs to come to terms with hating her baby for making impossible demands on her and not feel guilty about harbouring such feelings. Similarly, staff working with extremely demanding patients or clients can also 'hate' them for not getting better or apparently not responding to their care. The patients, in fact, often set up or re-enact a similar scenario to the family environment, which made them ill in the first place – drawing staff into the original family dynamics.

Staff attend the staff support group with similar expectations of the facilitator: the hope is that she will tell them what to do and how to make things better. If she fails to do this, she may be attacked or denigrated and the bad feelings can be dumped in her. Alternatively, she may be idealised and seen to have good ideas and to think in a way they cannot. Their own capacity to think may have been affected by their immersion in a chaotic and psychotic environment. They then feel powerless having idealised the facilitator who becomes powerful (in fantasy). Perhaps I am also envied for being able to leave the group when the hour is up, whereas they have to return into the ward and get on with the tough work of caring.

MANAGING MY OWN IDEALISM/REALISM BALANCE

The journey from idealism to realism inevitably has to deal with not just denigration but disillusionment. Disillusionment is not the same as cynicism, which is often a reaction to disappointment. The process of disillusionment is inevitable as we learn to accept that we are only human and can be vulnerable at times of stress and certainly not infallible.

As a staff group facilitator for many years I have had to learn my own limitations and also how to manage my own boundaries. Sometimes I am aware of attempts to push or pull me across a boundary in order to meet a group or individual's (unconscious) needs e.g. asking me an inappropriate personal question as the group finishes and I am getting up to leave. There may be various reasons for this: perhaps to test my strength and authority or perhaps in the hope of befriending me. I need to be clear and honest in my reactions to such events and help people understand the limits of my professional relationship with them.

My idealism is sustained by the people I meet in the groups I facilitate, because of their commitment and dedication in the face of ever decreasing resources, particularly in the public sector. My realism is an acceptance and awareness of my own and others' limits.

THE SUPERWOMAN SYNDROME

Example

A team in a well-established voluntary agency working with troubled adolescents had a new consultant psychologist in a leadership role. Alison's initiation into the new service had been gruelling, having had to manage a number of critical events including the suicide of an adolescent.

The early signs accurately foretold how things were going to be for her. Difficult young people seemed to be lining up to present ever more disturbing forms of self-harm. A number of staff vacancies remained frozen; meanwhile, a service audit was critical of team working practices; and all of this was happening in the context of searching internal and external investigations into the suicide. She was feeling drained and tested to the limit.

This was happening in the context of an everyday job managing a treatment environment for highly disturbed patients (many of whom had failed to benefit from treatment regimes elsewhere). Thus she found herself 'sucked into' a high pressure situation, which she experienced as increasingly oppressive.

In one particular group session, Alison's mobile phone began to ring. We all jumped in surprise and the conversation was halted while she answered it rather than switch it off! This had never happened before, there being an unspoken rule that phones were always switched off. I commented on this intrusion into our group (my own annoyance was transparent) and challenged her need to have the phone on 24 hours a day. At this, she burst into tears and shared her distress with us. She spoke movingly about the various demands being made on her, including working too many hours at great cost to her personal life. By bringing her mobile phone with her into our group we had been made to experience an unwelcome intrusion into our space which mirrored her own situation.

In the ensuing discussion, the team noted that previous leaders had said very similar things. And, quickly, there emerged the image of a 'vortex', (sucking people into a place of no return, where one takes on other people's jobs and concerns in order to feel useful and to matter). Indeed, the 'vortex' soon came to be tangibly located in the nurses' office.

As the debate unfolded, focus came on the relationship between the internal pressures and motivations and the external ones which play havoc with our boundaries. How far can you be pushed by a crisis situation into taking on 'too much'?

What is at stake here?

A number of *external pressures* may be at play such as a lack of resources, crises which take immediate attention, or a mis-management of resources.

However, there are also *internal pressures*, the driving forces behind our decisions to do what we do come from experiences earlier in our lives. We may have been relied upon in our families to carry the emotional burdens, and this may have contributed to us feeling we are good at rescuing situations in times of crisis. The notion of 'saving' leads us to feel potent and in control, illusory though that feeling may be. The wish to be indispensable or irreplaceable is strong and may lead to the superwoman (or man!) syndrome!

We have to work out how to create and protect boundaries that protect us from too much impingement which result in time off with 'stress' sickness. There has to be an agreement with oneself about this from early on, otherwise if there are no rules then anything is possible. If people know you can be pushed, they will push you!

If we accept the proposition that (conscious and unconscious) processes *within* people shape the relationships *between* them, then we have to allow the possibility of disturbed staff relationships occurring in environments where the work is with regressed individuals.

It has long been known that staff pathology is intimately interwoven with that of the patients. In particular, Main called attention to what he called 'special patients' (Main 1957: 138), a group that elicited a response of unusual involvement and closeness from staff, including sharp divisions of opinion, with some staff advocating strongly on behalf of particular patients, whereas others were only in touch with the negative qualities of these same patients.

Vignette: ignoring the time boundary and becoming ill

This is the story of a brief, focused intervention with a community child health team in a busy, provincial city. It was at the heart of a complex network focused on our most ill and disabled children, some of whom were in the process of dying. A focused intervention is a time limited number of sessions to address a specific issue. Usually this is addressed using a brief consultation to the team. In some circumstances 'the issue' is a symptom of an underlying dynamic that as in this case is more appropriately dealt with in a long-term staff support group.

The team found itself with some persistently difficult dynamics and asked for help. The work of the team was with children (and their families) where severe developmental difficulties (physical, cognitive and emotional) pre-dominated. The team was comprised of a group of able, highly committed individuals led by a deeply caring and charismatic male consultant.

The persistent difficulty within this staff group was an emergent pattern whereby one of the staff would become ill and/or leave 'badly', all of this being 'unsayable' or 'undiscussable' within the team.

This staff group had an interesting attitude to the time boundary that I believe illustrated their collective wish to create hope where there was none or at any rate very little. It also reflected their struggle with being imbued with omnipotence by the parents when they actually felt impotent especially in the more difficult cases. They appeared to pay no attention to the time allowed for each session as if the amount of time they had was infinite and I found it very difficult to bring my consultation sessions with them to an end.

On the surface, there was a natural tendency towards a positive attitude in dealing with the realities of each child's difficulties and each parent's fears and to exercise 'damage limitation'. The negative or more disturbing areas were avoided for fear of upsetting the parents/staff even more; but this avoidance had a destructive aspect in not allowing staff a clear balanced and realistic appraisal of their work. In such situations, these problematic feelings do not just 'disappear'; they go somewhere and then they erupt through the surface in inconvenient ways and at inconvenient times.

These very uncomfortable feelings, such as guilt, despair, stress and anxiety, seemed to find a location in a particular crisis issue or staff member who had a propensity to take on the feelings. The staff member acts as a container, according to their own history and psychopathology, and rather like a psychic sponge mops up the messy feelings and carries them with inevitable conse- quences such as illness or acting out of one kind or another e.g. aggressive outbursts/lateness/crisis.

One staff member, who had left 'badly', leaving the staff team frustrated and angry, came to be seen as the 'unhelpable member'. She seemed to reflect and carry an 'unhelpable' aspect of the team. She had come to represent 'unfinished business' and came to be seen as a casualty from the last time the team had brought in an outside consultant.

As I worked with this team my own counter-transference feelings were a strong sense of failure in being able to tackle the underlying issues. I spoke about this with them. (By counter-transference, I mean those feelings which are not mine but those of the team, which I experience.) As the facilitator, I act as a container for these difficult feelings. Sometimes, I have to carry these feelings for several sessions until we reach a timely point in the group where I sense they are ready to acknowledge and discuss them.

As the team explored these issues with me, the understanding of them and subsequent resolution evoked a sense of power and hope in the group and a strong feeling of a burden being lifted that had lain heavily with them. The realisation that they needed to look after themselves more efficiently created the opportunity of organising individual mentors for the team. They did not in this case want to pursue a staff support group.

CONCLUSION

The central idea of this chapter was that of managing personal and pro- fessional boundaries between individuals and in groups. I have suggested (and demonstrated via vignettes and case illustrations) that there is often a fine line between these boundaries. The role of the facilitator is to 'patrol' these individual and group boundaries in the sense of being vigilant at all times as to how and when these boundaries are being used or abused (Barnes *et al.* 1999: 85).

There are some circumstances when it is appropriate to cross the boundary by seeing people individually. It is more of an extension of the group boundary around the individual to help bring in a difficult issue, or the person into the group. It prevents it from being separate and something that can not be discussed. People's personal situations do cross the boundary into the group, and they also influence their ability to maintain their own personal boundaries.

An interplay of external and internal pressures creates a force field around the boundary where overwhelming needs of one kind or another (narcissistic/ primitive/sexual/infantile to name but a few) can lead to inappropriate relationships between staff and patients, and other types of acting out such as leaving abruptly, becoming ill or working overlong hours and all the other situations mentioned in this chapter.

The external boundaries of the group are maintained by attention to punctuality, regular membership and behaviour in the group. Internal boundaries require a space for thoughtful response rather than simple reaction. By considering and talking about, for example, how feelings influence the way staff relate to patients, inappropriate relationships can be avoided. In the same vein, I have to consider the meaning of my own feelings and their influence on my interventions.

An understanding and increased awareness of personal motivation for becoming a health professional serves to enhance and enrich the work and discourages potentially abusive situations. It also increases the likelihood of establishing a realistic approach to the work, helping the worker to be clear as to what is possible and what is not and counter-balancing idealisation of the care task.

One hopes that the worker can find a way to use his/her self as a therapeutic instrument while at the same time being able to maintain their personal integrity. The ways to do this are through increasing self-awareness (and organisational self-awareness), through undertaking personal therapy, individual and/or group supervision, and finding time for reflective spaces in the work with the team, either with or without an external consultant.

ACKNOWLEDGEMENT

Grateful thanks to Graeme Farquharson for his help and encouragement.

Chapter 13

Working with disturbed states of mind

Nick Humphreys

EDITORS' INTRODUCTION

As in the chapter by Chris Powell, Humphreys writes from the position of a senior staff member acting as facilitator in the staff group within his own organisation. In this case the group is already well established, and Humphreys shares his thoughts and his interventions relating to two detailed examples, illustrating several aspects of the facilitator's role discussed in Chapter 5. He shows the importance of maintaining a sense of safety in helping the group to get on with its task of understanding, illustrates the appropriate use of self-disclosure, comments on parallel process between the staff and patient groups, and introduces some theory about the impact of working with victims of sexual abuse. This chapter illustrates the flexibility of staff support groups, described in Chapter 1, to meet a number of different needs.

This chapter is an attempt to give some clarity to a problem endemic to therapeutic communities, and to other settings that provide group therapies for patients struggling with high levels of disturbance and distress. The problem might be thought of as a psychological infection disturbing the shared thinking of the staff team or infiltrating the structure of the organisation. It is a problem that makes a serious contribution to defensive practice in staff teams.

A team's effective availability to a disturbed patient group as an instrument of therapy is comparable to the parental task of providing a safe physical and emotional environment for an infant. The maintenance of such a relationship is difficult. The psychological impact of the disturbance on a staff group can lead to staff unwittingly building barriers in the face of their intention to be receptive and emotionally available. The barrier may manifest as tiredness, disinterest, or lack of curiosity, disillusionment or boredom. Or it may drive overactivity, impulsiveness, or continual need for change. Such emotionally based responses, although disturbing, can often prove to be a helpful tool in understanding the group's emotional experience.

THE CONTEXT

The therapeutic community, whose staff group is the object of this study, is a long established organisation in an NHS setting. It provides a residential and a day service for mostly young people, men and women, many of whom have had lengthy and troubled relationships with general practice and psychiatry. They are frequently survivors of severe trauma who attract labels of personality disorder and who regulate their tendency to feel over-whelmed by acting out their distress. This means that although many have the potential to benefit from psychotherapy, they are unable to do so without the structural containment of the rules, routines and daily rhythms of the therapeutic community. It follows that if staff are to consistently provide such a service, they will require support and effective clinical supervision.

This is provided by a three tiered structure.

- Daily informal, peer group supervision via staff handovers and brief, 20 minute 'after-group' discussions.
- A weekly one-hour staff group that meets without an external facilitator and which the whole clinical team is encouraged to attend.
- A quarterly team day with an external facilitator.

The structure aims to capture those issues that are most alive at each level. At the first level, the after-group discussion is concerned with the clinical task. At the second level the staff group is concerned with the relationship between the staff team and the clinical task and with working relationships within the team. At the third level the quarterly team day provides access to the broadest view of the overall task, including the political dimension of the relationship between the service and the wider organisation of the trust.

At the time of this study the team had to manage the impact of con-siderable change stemming from the NHS modernisation agenda, from service developments, from efficiency savings in the trust, and from changes of personnel within the staff team. Some senior members of the team had left and with an influx of new posts and new blood, there was both a renewal of enthusiasm and creativity and a tendency towards a strained cultural divide between the old and the new.

Into this fertile but vulnerable situation there came over the course of several weeks, disclosures within the patient group about trauma, parti-cularly about sexual abuse. There appeared to be a correspondence between the disclosures and a subsequent increase in defensive practice in the team.

This took the form of either manifest conflict in the staff group or a peculiar malaise, which affected the work as a whole. The links between the dynamics of the staff team and the patient group were not at all obvious and the situation was difficult to observe. The team was aware that as much as it was alert in theory to the importance of its continuing availability to the community during a turbulent time, it was also struggling to prevent its therapeutic alliance with the patient group deteriorating into what might be called a 'getting by' alliance. This was expressed for the team by a staff member who said that what she wanted to be able to do was to come to work, do her job and go home again without having to think about work all the time when she was not on duty.

I am going to use vignettes taken from two staff groups to illustrate and think about the problem that I have called an infection in the psychological structure of the organisation. I am writing from the viewpoint of the senior member of staff in each group. This is not a clearly defined role. It does not involve working as a designated facilitator, but straddles a space between an implicit expectation of leadership and of functioning as a member of the team. It is a role taken not exclusively by myself but also by other senior team members at other times. Although we aim for a consistency of approach, the work inevitably reflects the strengths and weaknesses of different personalities and styles of intervention. The following therefore reflects the bias of my own method: a mixture of facilitation and supervision tailored to working in a group context. My theoretical orientation is best described as psychoanalytic. A little later I will draw attention to my experience of the advantages and disadvantages of the informality of the role.

Staff Group One

During this phase in the life of the community, the subject matter of the staff group was dominated by an anxious awareness in the team of the extensive disclosures about sexual abuse. The work of the group involved communicating about and digesting the emotional and psychological burden. The following scenario is from a staff group meeting that typified for the team the emergence of a destructive force that was difficult to reckon with. The meeting started in a state of some anxiety because word had already got round that Anna, one of the unit's doctor's, was going to confront Brian, another doctor, about a particular patient's prescription. Anna had made it clear in a community meeting that she was not willing to re-write an 'as required' prescription. She had a difficult relationship with the patient concerned. Brian on the other hand had responded to the same patient's appeal for understanding, had previously agreed that the patient should be allowed 'as required' medication and had informed the team that the patient had agreed to use this judiciously. Brian was angry that his relationship with the patient had been undermined and thought Anna should have consulted him before she made her decision.

At the very start of the group Brian quite powerfully expressed his grievance. Called upon to justify her decision not to write the prescription, Anna at first struggled to gather her thoughts, but went on to present a rationale that showed up a side to the patient that Brian seemed less acquainted with. It seemed as though the discussion was about to become more shared and helpful when Brian took it in a different direction by suggesting Anna would benefit from developing a more informal social relationship with the patients. Anna looked mortified and then became upset. It was evident to everyone that Anna was experiencing some difficulty adapting to the therapeutic culture of the group, but Brian's comment seemed to have triggered a personal issue for Anna. The team's silent but apparent discomfort increased, as Brian seemed irritated rather than troubled by Anna's distress.

I said I thought we should pause and try to think together about what was happening. I thought it was important to call a halt to a process that had become destructive and that this needed to be demonstrated because we would not be able to think together unless we could retrieve a sense of safety. (Whenever communication becomes persecutory like this it is difficult to think and reflect.) I thought an issue about power, a motivation to exercise power, had been evident in Brian's suggestion that Anna ought to develop her social relationship with the patients. I thought it had been untimely and invasive.

I was also aware that part of the backcloth to this conflict was a failure throughout the team, not only between the doctors, to address the communication problem. Both doctors had separately consulted the rest of the team about their respective decisions but the team had not managed to bring these communications together in its shared thinking. I thought the difficulty between the doctors could not be properly understood by treating it only at the level of a personal issue. I therefore intervened with a further comment directed to all of us, with the intention of relieving the pressure and making room to differentiate between the personal and the group collective level. I suggested that if we stepped back from the immediacy of the conflict we might see that some of the things that were happening were also happening in the patient group at the moment. I gave as examples the pattern of conflict whereby the group divided into oppositional subgroups, or one member attacked another under the voyeuristic gaze of the rest of the group, or an intervention that set out to be fair and balanced, either turned into, or was experienced as, a humiliating attack. Pointing to the pattern rather than the content of what was happening in the staff group, involved everyone. This was important because the group had divided into protagonists and observers. It also linked the staff group to the group as a whole: staff and patients.

A still anxious but more reflective discussion ensued. The team was able to ask itself why the medication issue had not been more straightforwardly resolved and one or two members realised they could probably have helped Brian and Anna out at an informal level without directing the problem to the staff group. I said I felt we were struggling as a team to hold something together that felt just a bit too big and difficult. This was a vague thing to say but I wanted to get at the qualitative feel of the burden, to encourage further reflection. As it happened I think this was a slightly mis-timed intervention and on reflection I would say the team were not quite ready to make use of it. They were still feeling too unsafe and my comment raised rather than lowered anxiety. They wanted to know more about what I meant.

At this point I was aware of a problem about investment and idealisation. In part the team wanted to regress and trust itself to the mind of someone who would function as a rescuing figure and make things better. The presence of powerful destructive forces in the community drove the search for such a figure. Being on the receiving end of the projection was uncomfortable but not entirely avoidable. In my experience it is best to accept the projection and understand it but take care not to identify with it; that is, do not begin to believe you are what the group wants you to be. I therefore decided that I needed to negotiate between being active enough to promote safety but not so active that I would encourage the group's dependency.

I suggested that in various ways we might all be caught up with the community's current struggles. I then generalised with what I went on to say. I am sure there are limits to how helpful this can be, but in this instance I think it helped the team to locate its dilemma against the backcloth of a larger, typical picture. I suggested that working with disturbed states of mind involved having to manage and work with disturbance as it manifested in the daily life of the group. These manifestations might be thought of as dramatisations or re-enactments of patients' hidden experiences of suffering, and take place between individuals, or between an individual and the group, or between subgroups within the group. In an emotionally disturbed situation, such as our group that was working with disclosure about sexual abuse, we would inevitably find ourselves being shaped as participants to respond with a mindset and an emotional tone whose origin we could not quite be sure of. Then, I suggested, it was not uncommon for staff to find themselves saying or doing things that seem out of character, and that bewildering or as frankly unpleasant as such experiences could be, the therapeutic work was bound up with both being a part of them and managing to observe them. I suggested this might be a basis for trying to understand what had happened in our staff group, and that without this broader perspective the problem could only be attributed to the working relationship between the doctors, to the team's lack of clarity about dispensing medication or to the resident at the centre of the argument. These factors were both realities in their own right and agents that could be thought of as having been pulled into the service of a dramatisation about sexual abuse, the presiding trauma whose hidden but powerful dynamics had infiltrated the system. This was perhaps the loose cannon that could be thought of as having the team in its grip.

The staff group was then able to unpack this further. The spirit of enquiry was reflective rather than persecutory. We were able to fill the larger picture with more detail and this provided the ground against which the problem in the staff group could emerge in a new light. Brian apologised for the tack he had taken. Anna was able to speak about her anger and to note that one of the most painful aspects of the previous meeting had been the observing silence of the group. It had felt humiliating and as though she had been up against something absolutely immovable, quite as bad in its own way as Brian's implacability. Jean, one of the formerly silent members of the team, became upset, expressing some doubt about her capacity to work in the therapeutic community. Another member of the team, Diane, was more defensive in the face of Jean's distress. She said it had not been clear to anyone how the situation should have been managed and that the team required better guidelines for handling such situations in the future. At this point I again noted the similarities between this problem and the issues currently alive in the patient group: loss of confidence on the one hand, and on the other a movement towards regulation, a bureaucratisation of the life of the group. Someone said this might be about increased anxiety, an attempt to safeguard the group from the disorientating impact of abuse disclosures.

Mary, a new member of the team, said the staff seemed just as anxious as the patients and that as a newcomer it made her more anxious than having to hear disclosures about abuse. She suggested that if she was feeling that, then perhaps patients were too. This comment had the effect of turning the tables because it helped the team to realise it had mostly been considering the impact of the patient group on itself. I said I imagined the patient group could only be as healthy as we were as a staff group. The idea of a reciprocal relationship involving communication of disturbance from the patient group, difficulty with its management in the staff group, and subsequent anxiety and defensiveness in both groups, helped the team to imaginatively compare what was happening to the effect of trauma on a family. For example, Jean suggested the situation that Diane wanted guidelines for managing was comparable to the dreadful situations that our abused patients had found themselves in. I thought this idea could be extended to look at what had happened in the group, and that the group was now safe enough to return to the content. I therefore pointed to three strands of the drama: first that Brian had unwittingly acted into the role of an intrusive, abusive figure, who exploited Anna's vulnerability; second, that Anna had correspondingly experienced the feelings of the abused victim, feelings of shame and humiliation and a sense of powerlessness; third, although the team had also struggled with feelings of helplessness, it had perhaps been experienced by Anna as the other parent who could potentially have protected the child, but chose instead to turn a blind eye.

This was particularly difficult for those members of the group who felt they had been the unwitting observers of a drama they had felt powerless to intervene in. Judy, who had been one of the silent observers, commented: 'By the time I realised I was involved and perhaps ought to be doing something it felt too late. I didn't know how to intervene or what to say.' She said that seeing her personal failure, as a key to getting a handle on the appalling failure of care in patients' lives, was however a helpful thought. This in turn allowed someone else to say she felt she had let both doctors down because she had had no idea how to intervene. The meeting was later described as healing. The following is a summary of its salient features.

The team was able to move from an anxious and persecuted position to make an observation about its own functioning when I was able to help it to find a reflection of itself in the patient group. Mary capitalised on this point by using her own experience to empathically consider what patients might be feeling. I felt my comment was facilitative by virtue of providing some direction that the team was in need of, but also through being open: framed as a piece of curiosity that required the team's further thinking. In subsequent discussion the impact of Mary's comment about patients feeling anxious about the staff, was understood in terms of helping to re-humanise the team's relation to the patient group. It had the effect of dispelling a myth in the mind of the team that had begun to shape the team's relation to the patient group. This myth consisted of an unconscious idea by which the patients were perceived as an enemy to be defended against. Clearly some reparative movement had taken place, enabling Brian to make way for what followed with his apology. The key to the freeing up of communication and the resumption of creative thinking was located in the team's discovery of the latent problem beneath the manifest difficulty. It was this perspective that enabled Judy to think about her personal failure in a new light. Starting to grapple with the elements of the dramatisation the team had been caught up in was helpful because seeing themselves as part of a larger picture that could never be entirely known helped staff to feel less anxious and defensive about their failures and the seeming inadequacy of their interventions. Maximising the spirit of reflective enquiry was achieved by ensuring that individual staff were not considered in isolation but in the context of the group as a whole. The team was able to reflect on how demoralised it had become in the face of its basic wish to be helpful, as well as how easily we could fall prey to omnipotence − a wish to be all healing and all helpful. One reason that this happens as readily as it does in work with high levels of disturbance and distress is that it can be very difficult to work with the reality of lasting damage and still retain a sense of therapeutic efficacy. The staff group was able to acknowledge how difficult much of the sexual abuse material was to listen to, how difficult it was not to feel angry with patients for continuing to talk about it, and how appalled the team felt by the stark realty of abuse. Although it was sobering to think that some of our patients might never be able to get better, the thought also helped the team to sharpen its sense of the work task and define the limits of its responsibility.

Staff Group Two

This vignette is taken from a staff group where the subject of scrutiny was the seemingly endless dissatisfaction in the team with the staff lunch break. The root of the difficulty was similar to the problem in the first vignette, but in this case part of the organisational structure of the unit had turned into a stage for an enactment.

The original idea had been that once weekly the whole team should meet for lunch in a designated room in the unit. It became a subject for discussion in the staff group when the problems with it began to look like more than teething troubles. The discussion sounded a note of exasperation directed towards our apparent inability to nurture and feed ourselves in a straight-forward way.

There were complaints about there not always being enough money in the kitty; about some staff ending up out of pocket; about uncertainty about who would be present; about how much food would be needed; about what to buy and about some staff having to shop more frequently than others.

Some team members would be late for the lunch and there would be little left; or worse, they would have been forgotten. Some struggled with what they felt was the self-gratifying task of preparing a meal from which the patients were excluded, whereas others asserted their right to time out, talked about modelling self-care or compared the situation to parents having quality time alone. The meal was described as sitting round in a large group crunching bread and lettuce, and feeling like you had to be on your best behaviour.

I said I thought there was something interminable about the discussion and there were comments about going round in circles whenever we talked about it. I said I thought there must be something about the process that was significant. What could having so much to say that did not lead us anywhere mean to us?

Some people said they hated the room we were using and that it might feel better if music was playing. Another suggestion was that it would feel easier in small groups rather than one large one. I said I thought this was another variation on the same theme and that we might do better trying to think about how we were using the lunch break rather than what was wrong with it. I realised that beneath the problem of our apparent attempts to find a solution we were becoming anxious about our relationships with one another and worried that we were unable to relax together in a setting we had created for the express purpose of relaxing together.

One member said he could hardly remember the last time he had taken part in the lunch break when it had not been filled with a peculiar tension that only perpetuated divisions and disharmonies rather than brought the team together. He thought there was something to be considered about the idea of using our dissatisfaction with the lunch break to maintain a state of impasse. Although we needed more information about why we should want to invest in being stuck, I sensed how reluctant we were to pick this idea up. The reluctance seemed to support the view that had been expressed. At this point it would have been easy to side with the one helpful thought about the function of the lunch break, but I thought this would risk creating a division, which would simply repeat the problem of divisiveness and further obscure reflection and thinking. Therefore, although I did not at this point quite understand our defensiveness, I felt a general comment about our work with the patient group might by-pass the defence and help us to think about what we were doing.

At length I made a comment that had an impact comparable to Mary's remarks in the first vignette where she had made an observation based on an empathic identification with the patient group. It ran something like this:

> I suggested that if something like this was going on in the patient group, if they were absenting themselves, or creating as much chaos around an issue as we appeared to be doing around our lunch break, we would not be hesitating to ask what was going on.

As I was speaking I felt I was at risk of being critical, but it seemed to help one member to express her anger and disappointment with the lunch break. She felt we had not stepped back to consider there might be a problem about creating a structure concerned with food and feeding in a context where the problem of maternal deprivation was never far away. She said that trying to take time out from the work task in the workplace, was like digging a large hole at the side of a raging torrent and getting into it with an expectation of staying dry.

This was a helpful metaphor, enabling the group to gradually find its way to the latent issue behind the manifest problem and to focus more on the possible meaning of its behaviour. Using my colleague's image of trying to create a protected space in a situation that was least likely to sustain it, I shared my own experience of shopping for the staff lunch.

I recalled my sense of feeling dull and tired and the odd thought that what I was buying would be merely eaten. I imagined there would be no thanks, that my effort would not be appreciated. It was a lifeless, depressing, emotionally devoid provider–consumer relationship. I suggested it was a state of mind that belonged more to the psychology of the patient group where there had been so much experience of damaged people emptying themselves in their attempts to make their parents better, attempts that always failed. I said our lunch break seemed to have been hijacked by a dramatisation of the psychology of a group that was defending against awareness of the enormity of its need, its envy and its despair about being able to have anything good.

Inadvertently it seemed that we had created a powerful arena emotionally linked to the task of mothering, and forming thereby, an emotional highway to our patients' deepest concerns, which through our behaviour, we had acted out.

Uncovering the latent issue behind the manifest problem – once again the impact of the patient group's disturbance on the team's capacity to function effectively – enabled the team to be less concerned with what it was doing wrong and more interested in the meaning of its behaviour. Our attempt to segregate ourselves from the work task had unconsciously connected us to it at greater depth.

FACILITATION AND STRUCTURE

The structure of my role within the team had an important bearing on my ability to work with sufficient objectivity in each group. My clinical role in the unit was limited to attending community meetings – daily large group meetings where all patients and staff on duty would attend. This enabled me to achieve a general overview of the psychodynamic life of the community, which was useful to the staff group because it put me in a good position to contextualise and comment on emergent issues in the more focused areas of the clinical work.

However, the position of senior team member acting as facilitator was not without its difficulties. My experience was that it created certain defensive problems. Over and against the task of achieving a balancing act between being sufficiently inside to understand subjectively and far enough outside to understand objectively, there were attempts to 'fix' my role. That is at one extreme there was a subtle and disempowering pressure for me to enter more fully into the defensive life of the staff group. I felt this was more evident in the psychodynamics of the second vignette where a persuasive pull to collude with an organisational defence was operative. At the other extreme was a push for me to function more on the outside. Idealisation, which I have already mentioned in respect of the first vignette, was a driver for this. Each extreme of objectification demands a tolerance of others' distorted perceptions of one, and is a challenge to a facilitator whether he or she is external to the staff group or internal to it. I would suggest that in my position it was more onerous because it went hand in hand with the necessity of maintaining a daily working relationship with the staff team. My own defensive inclination was to gravitate too far in or too far out because this meant less uncertainty and therefore less anxiety.

One further problem about functioning as an internal facilitator was that I could never quite be contained within the team as a whole and this inevitably left me with certain blind spots. For example, although being inside the staff group gave me a greater sensitivity to its experience of itself, there were also parts of that experience that were harder for me to observe just because I too was part of it. I could never quite see the staff group beyond the bias of my own experience of it, and I think the staff group could never wholly see itself through me because it had a working relationship with me that coloured its perceptions.

CONCLUSION

What I hope these examples reveal is that part of the inherent difficulty of the work is that beyond a certain point of intensity the impact of the patient group is unconsciously experienced as toxic and something to be defended against. Empathy is a challenge because it will often take us to places we would rather not go to, and yet, one way or another, our patients will find out whether we are able to accompany them through the use of our own emotional experience. What can so easily emerge as our own failings almost always hold elements that have a vital contribution to make to a fuller understanding of the situation. In both vignettes the resolution depended on our ability to penetrate our personal difficulties to find something beyond the level of the personal, and which our personal proclivity was in fact allowing us to hold for the group as a whole.

Chapter 14

Working with staff dynamics in an educational setting: the staff support group that wasn't to be

Gary Winship

EDITORS' INTRODUCTION

In this final chapter Gary Winship explores the question of staff support for teachers, and presents his initial meeting with the staff of a school following a number of incidents of self-harm, to discuss the offer of support. In Chapter 2 we examined some of the difficulties staff have in asking for or accepting support, and here we see how areas of potential conflict and rivalry within a team, and rejection of the need for support by some members, can put a brake on the school taking up Winship's offer. The chapter highlights the importance of the initial request in setting up a support group – which we explore in Chapter 4 – in particular knowing why the request is coming from a particular person in the organisation and the support it has from the head of the organisation. Winship also reflects on the details involved in managing feelings of anxiety and the need for safety in a first meeting with a staff group. It may be a suitable cautionary note to end on.

Support or sensitivity?

The agenda for emotional well-being in schools is currently shaping the aspirations for schools' improvement where there is momentum to re-create schools as a frontline of primary health care. The establishment of staff support groups in schools, led by psychologically qualified practitioners, could add a new dimension to the repertoire of efforts aimed at increasing workforce well-being, as well as offering a way of increasing teachers' psychological mindedness about pupil well-being. This, at least, was the start point for my consultation with a school where there had been a spate of self-harm among pupils. I ought to say from the outset that the idea of 'support', and support for a 'group' of teachers, might have given me more cause for reflection. I have discovered before that the term 'staff support group' can be misleading. For instance in research carried out by colleagues participating in a staff support group in an NHS inpatient psychiatric unit, on average less than 10 per cent of the group session was found to be 'supportive' according to participants (Winship and Hardy 1999). The question was: 'what constituted the other 90 per cent of the group experience?' The research highlighted that the majority of the time was felt to be taken up by interpersonal conflicts, clinical de-briefing and managing a bothersome range of unwanted emotions like anger and hostility, resentment, rivalries and so forth. Nevertheless, the group was valued by many staff and felt to be an integral part of the emotional circuit training for new staff and a place for 'psychic detoxification', or de-briefing, for more experienced staff.

After the research findings were circulated to the staff team it was decided that the term 'staff sensitivity group' was more able to convey the array of experiences contained within the group, and less likely to lead to disappointment for new staff who might be expecting the group to be supportive. That is not to say that this particular staff 'support group' did not foster support. Anecdotally at least, the group seemed to acclimatise a milieu of support among colleagues, albeit mostly after the group had ended. Although the group itself may not have been supportive, it seemed to have a purpose in creating a therapeutic community beyond the group. The group sensitised participants to the need for support among colleagues in the days or week ahead.

I mention this in relation to my vignette of a school consultation where my remit was that of considering how to support teachers in managing self-harming pupils. Had my task been that of addressing the question as to 'how the teachers might become more sensitive to the reality of pupil self-harm', I might have been more successful. Ultimately, my recommendation that the school set up a 'staff support' group did not get followed through. So I have cause to reflect on an instance where, in spite of my best efforts, there was a less favourable outcome than might have been hoped for. I am left to reflect on the possibility that the teachers did not find my initial group consultation very supportive. The idea that the group experience, like the consultation which had been a taster for a support group, should be installed on a regular basis was resisted. It is certainly not my want to quell the passions of resistance and there may have been other reasons for not starting a staff group. It is a shame that the opportunity for the staff team to increase their emotional literacy was missed. It is with this in mind, that I reflect from the perspective of a psychoanalytic humanistic approach on the uncommon challenge of staff support groups for teachers in schools.

CONTEXT TO VIGNETTE: EMOTIONAL WELL-BEING IN SCHOOLS

The well-being agenda in schools has begun to shape aspects of educational policy and practice. Although the idea of physical or food related well-being of school children has been profiled, emotional or mental well-being has featured rather less. Yet the British Medical Association (BMA 2006) has drawn attention to the prevalence of child and adolescent mental heath disorders highlighting that at any one time in the UK, one in ten children under the age of sixteen has a mental health illness.[1] Presentation of mental health problems in childhood are reliable predictors for enduring and more severe mental health problem in adolescence and adulthood (Chen et al. 2006; Sourander et al. 2006), so early intervention here would seem indicated. The call for teachers to develop faculties for recognizing and responding to psychological distress would seem to arise out of this need to ensure that schools optimise the opportunity for early years well-being as a root for lifetime health.

Recognition of the psychological needs of the teacher might be a precursor to the well-being of the pupils. This has been the base assumption of my work, and that of others, with staff groups in mental health institutions (Barnes et al. 1998; Haigh 2000; Hardy et al. 1998; Winship 1995; Winship and Hardy 1999). I begin working with a staff group with an understanding that the capacity of the staff to offer emotional support to patients is proportionate to the psychological support they themselves experience. This is the challenge of establishing a process of psychological support for any professional emotional labour.

Early findings from a six-year longitudinal research study at University of Nottingham, the 'On Becoming a Teacher' (BaT) project, suggest that new teachers in particular do identify a need for ongoing psychological support beyond the initial phase of early career mentorship (Hobson et al. 2007). However, descriptions as to what form this psychological support might take are lacking. The absence of interventions may be the result of the fact that, as Day et al. (2007) point out, alertness to the need for emotional awareness among teachers is only recently acknowledged. The following vignette offers an account of a staff group consultation where some of these issues came into focus.

---

1 The BMA report also drew attention to the fact that British young people were involved in more violence, drug taking and binge drinking than teenagers in other European countries and that 168,000 11–15-year-olds will abuse glue and solvents in a year. The report noted that one in five girls aged 15–17 engage in self-harm, with an average age onset of 12. Bullying was likewise found to be prevalent with a third of all boys and a quarter of all girls bullying other children at some time during their school career. The report concluded that dedicated services for children and young people were scant and that many GPs ended up being forced to prescribe antidepressants (to over 40,000 children in the UK) against National Institute for Health and Clinical Excellence (NICE) guidelines because waiting lists for psychological therapies were so long.

Case vignette

Following concern about a spate of self-harm among pupils in a large independent day and boarding school for 11–18 year olds, I was invited by the school nurse, who had heard about my work and range of interests through my university work, to come and speak to the teachers. I was asked to consider ways in which the teachers might be supported in their work. At the consultation there were 20 teachers in attendance. The meeting was held in a large room overlooking the school's extensive playing fields. I judged the room to be large enough to comfortably accommodate the staff in a large oval, so I laid out the chairs accordingly prior the meeting.

The meeting began on time and I opened with a brief summary of my background in the NHS working with self-harmers, people suffering from depression and my experience of working with young substance misusers. I outlined my expectations for the session that was scheduled for one and half hours. I explained that I was not quite sure how I was going to help, but that I would offer some thoughts of my own based on my work with self-harming patients. But in the first place, I said I wanted to hear about their experiences. I suggested that we go around the group and that everyone check-in, first with their name, and then with a brief account of their experiences of dealing with self-harm, both in the current school and before. I felt that this suggestion was not entirely met with enthusiasm, but several heads nodded. After a few moments hesitation, I volunteered someone on my left to start the introductions. Initially the atmosphere of the check-ins was mixed with attentiveness and distraction, some staff were listening and looking whereas others were gazing at the floor or out of the window. Three male teachers held a not so hushed conversation with each other during the check-in. Although this atmosphere did not necessarily feel out of keeping with my experiences in medium to large groups where discussions can often be fractured, I felt that the number of staff initially attentive and enthused by the check-in seemed in the balance with those who felt to the contrary.

The initial timbre of the check-ins, characterised by anxiety and hesitancy, suggested that some staff felt uncomfortable about speaking either in the group, or about the topic; I was unsure which. The unfamiliarity of speaking in front of colleagues in the face-to-face encounter of the large group oval was probably discomforting. I also wondered how many staff were attending because they had been directed to, or whether it had been out of personal choice. Neither of these two questions that were in my mind did I speak out loud.

After several check-ins the tone of the group began to change. There was a far higher incidence of self-harm than I had anticipated, and there were a significant number of recent experiences, ranging from smoking, to cutting, to eating disorders and to a couple of students who had been expressing suicidal ideas. The atmosphere of the group seemed to become more seriously engaged, and there seemed to be less distracted attention. All but a few staff offered an account of direct contact with a self-harm incident within that last year. Some of the staff presented current concerns and dilemmas; encounters with cutting seemed strikingly prevalent and I began to wonder whether the school was experiencing some sort of contagious outbreak of cutting (something I have experienced elsewhere in the close knit environment of an inpatient ward).

During the check-in I made a few comments but tried not to interrupt the flow. The check-in lasted in the region of 45 minutes, with some people taking more time than others. Afterwards I reflected on the general themes that emerged and I offered some thoughts about the range of self-harming behaviours that the teachers had encountered. I talked about a spectrum model of self-harm, from the less serious to the more serious, and how counsellors and psychotherapists were usually keen to try and make sense of the self-harm as communication, a way of representing distress that could not be put into words. I talked in particular about cutting and how I understood cutting to sometimes be addictive and contagious, but again a way of expressing feelings where words were felt to have failed. I offered some thoughts on the different types of cutting; the relevance and meaning of which parts of the body are cut and so forth. Finally I turned to the question of suicide, and opened up some discussion which was engaged with keenly by several people. There were some common misunderstandings that I was able to tackle about, for instance, pseudo-suicide, and that people who say they are going to kill themselves are 'all talk' and less likely to kill themselves (of course not true), and that suicidal talk should be ignored as a plea for attention (the inverse being true, that attention needs to be offered). I presented some research about suicide risk factors and the task of risk assessment.

I was keen that my resume of information did not impinge too much on the group but I wanted to offer some food for thought. I opened up the question to the group about how they, as teachers, managed the self-harm they had described. Some of the older and more established masters who had worked at the school for a length, nonchalantly said they took self-harm to be 'no surprise' and 'part of the job'. This nonchalance was counterpoised by some of the newer staff, mostly female, who said they felt inadequately prepared during their training to deal with such events. One female member of staff became visibly distressed and said that she found it all very anxiety provoking, and she seemed to convey some resentment about the male staff who dismissed the issue. I commented about the emotional burden of the job, and said I wondered whether there were differences in how the men and women experienced this part of their job. I asked how the staff managed the difficult challenges of their work, I referred to the idea of 'emotional labour'. Four of the male masters said that they could always go down the pub, and this seemed to corner the conflict.

There did however, follow a keen discussion about how difficult the teachers found judging what acts of self-harm constituted a serious risk, and what might be normal adolescent experimentation such as smoking, drug-taking or experiments with food among girls. The discussion was insightful and I felt the need to say very little. I thought I detected the discussion had an atmosphere of relief, perhaps from the commonality of feelings and the apparent collective experience in the group. I suggested that in particular in regard to the boarding students the teachers seemed to be in the role of *in loco parentis*, that some of the difficult processes of adolescent transition, like rebellion and protest, were visited upon the teachers. Some of the teachers expressed strong hostility and resentment towards parents, expressing a feeling that they felt as if the children had been sent to the school because the parents could not bear to manage the emotional passage of adolescence.

As the group came to a close, I referred back to some of the early comments where some staff felt that they were inadequately prepared for the job, and that some extra support might be needed. I said that I felt the group had been a useful forum for expressing some difficult feelings. I drew parallels with staff working in mental health settings and that often staff groups were established with the remit of creating a space for support for staff. I suggested that the staff might consider the possibility of meeting on a regular basis to continue the discussions about self-harm. I further suggested that a frequency of monthly meetings seemed indicated and that it was something I would be interested to think about further with the group. The idea seemed to be welcomed by some of the group. A few weeks after the consultation I wrote to the school nurse and reiterated my suggestion of a monthly staff support group. I received a letter thanking me for the session but declining the offer of further meetings.

REFLECTIONS ON THE CONSULTATION

Hinshelwood's perspective on the role of external consultant as 'uncomfortably at variance with the dominant culture' (Hinshelwood 1994: 287) would seem apposite in the consultation above. The dominant culture seemed to be something akin to not speaking openly about self-harm. In the session this closed discourse was subverted from the opening of the group where I invited the teachers to talk about their experiences. The initial structure caused resistance and perhaps hostility and had I taken a different direction from the outset, a different atmosphere might have emerged. For instance I might have more carefully asked the group a simple opening question as to how they felt sitting in an oval. My act of setting out a circle of chairs had not been well received by some who might have been expecting a lecture style information dissemination session. The face-to-face setting was symbolic of an open structure that contrasted with the more familiar closed culture of not speaking about emotional matters.

Of course to some extent it is difficult for me to delineate what feelings I had accurately gleaned from the group, and what feelings simply arose from my own anxieties. My experience of working in many large staff groups with the aim of raising consciousness about how to manage and work more effectively with challenging aspects of human relations, suggests to me that the process of this group was not uncommon. That is to say, in the teacher group the manifestation of various tensions, resistances and rivalries in the group was commensurate with other large group settings I had encountered in mental health settings. I would also have expected, as was the case here, that as an external agent charged with some role of leadership or expertise, I would initially be a receptacle for an array of negative feelings in the group. And I think one of the first tensions in the group was to do with the dynamics of seniority and leadership. It is worth reflecting on the absence of the head teacher who did not attend the group, though again from my experience of participating in and running staff groups in the National Health Service it is not uncommon for senior staff to fail to attend a staff group. And where senior staff do attend, in about 75 per cent of cases their attendance dwindles over time. There seems to be a dissonance between how senior managers and junior staff perceive the function of the group. Managers may envisage the group to be a forum that will bring about coherence and reduction of workforce tension, whereas junior staff relish the opportunity to air grievances. These two functions may not be incompatible in the end, although it is often difficult for senior staff to experience the compression of hierarchy that is felt in a group situation. I have observed occasions when senior members of staff groups have withdrawn from the group and then have tried to close the group because they have felt that the discussions in the group have undermined the type of team coherence they hoped would be achieved at the outset. The group may find considerable energy in the absence of hierarchical leaders, and the group facilitator might feel implicated in the establishment of a sort of collective protest group that experiences some degree of triumph over the leadership.

The atmosphere of grievance apparent in the school staff group manifested itself in two ways; first in the disruption of some of the older male teachers, and then expressed in occasions of collective silence. It did seem to be potentially destabilising for the more established teachers to have the younger female teachers finding a voice to talk about their feelings. It was this difference between the men and women that seemed to suggest a second rivalry in the group. The rivalry seemed rather orthodox in as much as there seemed to be a patriarchal model of command and control that butted up against a more matriarchal model inclined towards meeting the challenge of emotional containment. The two dimensions of authority (male and female) may be inherently prone to opposing one another, although a group situation seems to offer a possibility that the bonds of rivalry might be superseded by a new affiliation disposed towards mutual authority. We might think about this in terms of transitions from 'paternalism' (father figure-head), to 'maternalism' (mother-head) to 'parentalism' (democratic parenting, shared executive). Certainly the horizontalities of a staff support are more inclined to create an inclusive space where the linear authority of male or female, father or mother, is superseded by the authority of the group (sometimes referred to as a higher power). The challenge in this case is embracing the verticalities of rivalry. That is to say, the staff support group may be an opportunity to consider and reflect on the authority structures in the group, including the authority of the facilitator. To some extent the initial consultation perhaps challenged the dominant culture whereby the senior masters who had worked at the school longer, were less able to dismiss the emotional agenda as the collective of voices were aired in the group.

CONCLUSIONS

On reflection perhaps I might have explored in more detail the background to the request, some consideration of the state of play between the health and education agendas in the school, the support of the senior staff for the invitation, an exploration of the likely attitudes of the school staff, and some thought as to what the expected outcome of the meeting might be. I am curious as to whether or not it would have been helpful for me to address the initial anxiety in the group about the unfamiliar challenge of just speaking in the group situation. I am not sure that by raising the issue initially I would have necessarily made the group feel safe and more comfortable. Indeed such scrutiny of process and immediacy might be felt to heighten anxiety initially. I have more lately been struck by the importance of disruption and fracture in the process of organisational progress (Winship 2005, 2007) and in this case the act of prompting self-scrutiny might have been discomforting. This is a tricky position for the external consultant who might be seen as subversive or undermining. I think there is something here about the duty of the consultant/facilitator to adopt an oppositional-critical stance, the challenge being that of presenting an alternative perspective to the organisation. In the case of drawing attention to the anxiety about the group process, it would be likely that some degree of consciousness-raising would have occurred illuminating the underlying anxiety. This anxiety was left dormant, possibly to exert more disturbance.

There may also be some question about the choice of seating arrangement. One option would have been to work with the space as it was upon arrival and allow the seating arrangements to emerge more organically, that is to say, allow participants to position their seats upon arrival, as and how they felt most comfortable. And I am left wondering if there might have been another way that I could have brought the session to close. My comparing the needs of the teacher group to that of a staff group in a mental health setting might have caused some alienation, irritation or anxiety that I might have been suggesting that the teachers might need therapy. The idea that the staff support situation in a school might resemble something of a therapeutic community system ought not to be dismissed. Indeed, in his work in establishing mental health interventions in schools, Graham Music (2007) argues that the array of complex institutional dynamics leads him to consider that the therapeutic community model of practice is relevant in formulating and intervening in the interlocking systems of in and out groups.

In the aftermath of the consultation and my written feedback suggesting an ongoing group, I might have responded more actively to the polite 'no thank you' reply. I was left feeling that the younger staff who had more ably expressed themselves had, in the end, been bullied by the older more reluctant team members. My recommendation that the staff repeat the uncomfortable experience on a regular basis was probably met with resistance. Nevertheless, I remain of the opinion that a staff group intervention might offer a consciousness-raising opportunity for teachers to learn about pupil well-being. The intervention may be effective without directly intruding upon the teacher–pupil milieu. In this way, the school milieu can avoid becoming a primary care psychiatric health setting with all of its possible pitfalls, while maintaining a close eye on pupil well-being.

The importance of working with staff as a first base to improving the lives of clients has been the basis of staff group work in mental health and psychiatry, and there is good reason to think that it might well offer new potential for improving the school milieu for teachers and pupils alike. The development of a curriculum for teaching emotional well-being to pupils might be a good idea, but it might also be precipitous without first ensuring that staff have been able to make sense of their own perspective and response to emotional distress and well-being.

Editors' conclusion

Problems are natural and should be expected. The underlying principle of this book is that they should not be ignored or avoided, and that managing them can be used as a learning experience for other problems in a team/group situation. Yet people are not naturally inclined to discuss with one another their feelings about the emotional impact of their work. They feel exposed and anxious and work is an environment that can be hostile to intimate conversations.

Staff support groups attempt to reconcile these two opposing forces – learning from experience versus anxiety over exposure to hostile reactions. This reconciliation is essential to the success of any support group, and we have attempted to identify some of the key steps a group facilitator can take to achieve it:

- ensuring the safety of the group setting, reliability and punctuality;
- not allowing people to feel isolated and encouraging identification and sharing;
- the facilitator addressing blocks to communications;
- managing the boundary of the group with the organisation.

The aim of the book is to provide a practical guide to the effective management and facilitation of staff support groups, and to the pitfalls that await the unprepared. In Part I of the book we focus in detail on the principles and practice of setting up and running staff support groups. Part II illustrates some of the difficulties and pitfalls as well as successes of staff support groups in different settings. Part II also provides examples of facilitators working within their own organisation as well as coming from outside; both have advantages and disadvantages, which require working with, and we do not make a recommendation that one is better than the other.

Both parts of the book look not only at what happens within the group but also at the relationship between the group and the organisation. A staff support group can be compared to a small craft on an organisational sea.

Under favourable conditions it can sail steadily and hold a lot of people, under difficult conditions it may manage to stay afloat with a few people, but under very poor conditions is likely to sink. Our book can be seen as a kind of guide both to boat building and to reading weather charts. If the boat is safe enough – well built and able to withstand squally conditions at times – it is more likely to be helpful to more people.

In the past, supervision and management were two areas of activity in health care settings that staff with a core professional training were often expected to undertake by virtue of their seniority and experience. Today there are recognized competencies and trainings in both these areas. We would argue that the same should apply to staff support groups. This raises the question of the relevant knowledge and skills. This is our initial list. We look forward to the first course to implement them.

Relevant knowledge:

- human social development, in particular attachment theory;
- psychodynamic concepts, in particular defence mechanisms, transference and counter-transference;
- social psychology of small groups and group dynamics;
- organisational and systems theory including decision-making processes.

Relevant skills:

- able to demonstrate empathic sensitivity; tolerance of high levels of anxiety in oneself and others;
- able to facilitate interaction in groups;
- able to recognize and manage boundary issues;
- able to negotiate with senior clinicians and managers.

As we pointed out in the introduction, this is the first book (that we know of) devoted to staff support groups in the helping professions. Producing a book is a risky business, particularly one that enters a new field, and as the editors we find ourselves feeling exposed. Are we on the right track? In keeping with our own principles, we would like to invite others to respond and contribute to this extremely important and, we believe, rewarding area of work, so that we can all learn from and build on each other's experience. A positive outcome of increased interest and study would be that staff support groups can work better for those who, research and anecdotes indicate, do not attend or benefit from them at present.

References

Agazarian, Y. M. (1997) *Systems-Centered Therapy for Groups.* New York: The Guildford Press.

Armstrong, D. (1995) The psychoanalytic approach to organisational life: why so little impact? *Group Analysis* 28: 33–45.

Armstrong, D. (2005) *The Organization in the Mind.* London: Karnac.

Ashton, T. (2007) Staff envy of the patients: A manifestation of this dynamic within a nephrology department in the setting of a general hospital. *Group Analysis* 40: 83–95.

Balint, M. (1968) *The Basic Fault: Therapeutic Aspects of Regression.* London: Tavistock.

Bamber, R. M. (2006) *CBT for Occupational Stress in Health Professionals: Introducing a Schema-focused Approach.* London: Routledge.

Barnes, B., Ernst, S. and Hyde, K. (1999) *An Introduction to Groupwork.* Basingstoke: Macmillan Press.

Barnes, E., Griffiths, P., Ord, J. and Wells, D. (1998) *Face to Face with Distress: The Professional Use of Self in Psychosocial Care.* London: Butterworth-Heinemann.

Bion, W. R. (1961) *Experiences in Groups.* New York: Basic Books.

Bolton, W. and Roberts, V. Z. (1994) Asking for help: staff support and sensitivity groups re-viewed. In A. Obholzer and V. Z. Roberts (eds) *The Unconscious at Work: Individual and Organisational Stress in the Human Services.* London: Routledge.

Booth, K. and Faulkner, A. (1986) Problems encountered in setting up support groups in nursing. *Nurse Education Today* 6: 244–51.

Borthwick, A., Holman, C., Kennard, D., McFetridge, M., Messruther, K. and Wilkes, J. (2001) The relevance of moral treatment to contemporary mental health care. *Journal of Mental Health* 10: 427–39.

Bram, P. J. and Katz, L. F. (1989) A study of burnout in nurses working in hospice and hospital oncology settings. *Oncology Nursing Forum* 16: 555–60.

Bramley, W. (1990) Staff sensitivity groups: A conductor's field experiences. *Group Analysis* 23: 301–16.

British Medical Association (2006) *Child and Adolescent Mental Health: A Guide for Healthcare Professionals.* London: BMA.

Brown, D. (2006) Dialogue for change. In J. Maratos (ed.) *Resonance and Reciprocity: Selected Papers by Dennis Brown.* Hove: Routledge.

Brown, D. and Pedder, J. (1979) *Introduction to Psychotherapy: An Outline of Psychodynamic Principles and Practice*. London: Routledge.

Bulman, C., Schutz, S. and Burns, S. (2004) *Reflective Practice in Nursing: The Growth of the Professional Practitioner*. Oxford: Blackwell.

Carsin, J., Fagin, L. and Ritter, S. (1995) *Stress and Coping in Mental Health Nursing*. London: Chapman and Hall.

Chen, H., Cohen, P., Kasen, S. and Johnson, G. (2006) Adolescent axis I and personality disorders predict quality of life during young adulthood. *Journal of Adolescent Health* 39: 14–19.

Craib, I. (1994) *The Importance of Disappointment*. London: Routledge.

Day, C., Sammons, P., Stobbart, G., Kington, A. and Gu, Q. (2007) *Teachers Matter*. Maidenhead: Open University Press/McGraw-Hill.

Department of Health (2000) *Improving Working Lives*. London: DH.

Department of Health (2002) *Mental Health Policy Implementation Guide: Adult Acute Inpatient Provision*. London: DH.

Department of Health (2003) *Improving Staff Morale*. London: DH.

Farquharson, G. (2003) Personal communication.

Ferguson, K., Owen, S. and Baguley, I. (2003) *The Clinical Activity of Mental Health Lecturers in Higher Education Institutions*. London: Department of Health report.

Foulkes, S. H. (1964) *Therapeutic Group Analysis*. London: Allen & Unwin.

Foulkes, S. H. (1975) *Group-analytic Psychotherapy: Method and Principles*. London: Gordon and Breach.

Glover, M. R. (1985) *The Retreat, York; An Early Experiment in the Treatment of Mental Illness*. York: William Sessions.

Haigh, R. (2000) Support systems 2. Staff sensitivity groups. *Advances in Psychiatric Treatment* 6: 312–19.

Hardy, S. E., Carson, J. and Thomas, B. (1998) *Professional Caring: Personal and Professional Approaches to Occupational Stress*. London: Stanley Thornes.

Harris, T. (1992) Some reflections on the process of social support and the nature of unsupportive behaviour. In H. O. F. Veiel and V. Bauman (eds) *The Meaning and Measurement of Social Support*. New York: Hemisphere Publishing.

Harvey, P. (1992) Staff support groups: are they necessary? *British Journal of Nursing* 1: 256–8.

Hawkins, P. and Shohet, R. (2000) *Supervision in the Helping Professions*, 2nd edn. Milton Keynes: Open University Press.

Hinshelwood, R. D. (1994) The relevance of psychotherapy. *Psychoanalytic Psychotherapy* 8: 283–94.

Hinshelwood, R. D. (2004) *Suffering Insanity: Psychoanalytic Essays on Psychosis*. London: Routledge.

Hinshelwood, R. D. (2008) Systems, culture and experience: Understanding the divide between the individual and the organisation. *Organisational and Social Dynamics* 8: 63–77.

Hinshelwood, R. D. and Skogstad, W. (2005) Observing organisations. Anxiety, defence and culture in healthcare. In R. D. Hinshelwood and W. Skogstad (eds) *Observing Organisations: Anxiety, Defence and Culture in Health Care*. London: Routledge.

Hirschhorn, L. (1993) *The Workplace Within*. Cambridge, Massachusetts: MIT Press.

Ho, D. (2007) Work discussion groups in clinical supervision in mental health nursing. *British Journal of Nursing* 16: 39–46.

Hobson, A. J., Malderez, A., Tracey, L., Homer, M., Mitchell, N., Biddulph, M., Giannakaki, M. S., Rose, A., Pell, R. G., Chambers, G. N., Roper, T. and Tomlinson, P. D. (2007) Newly Qualified Teachers' experiences of their first year of teaching: Findings from Phase III of the Becoming a Teacher project. Nottingham: Department for Children, Schools and Families (DCSF).

James, D. C. (1984) Bion's 'Containing' and Winnicott's 'Holding' in the context of the group matrix. *International Journal of Group Psychotherapy* 34: 201–13.

Kanas, N. (1986) Support groups for mental health staff. *International Journal of Group Psychotherapy* 36: 279–96.

Khaleelee, O. (1994) The defence mechanisms test as an aid for selection and development of staff. *Therapeutic Communities* 15: 15–33.

Lawrence, W. G. (1994) The politics of salvation and revelation in the practice of consultancy. In R. Casemore, G. Dyos, A. Eden, K. Kellner, J. McAuley and S. Moss (eds) *What Makes Consultancy Work – Understanding the Dynamics*. London: South Bank University Press.

Le Blanc, P. M., Hox, J. J., Schaufeli, W. B., Taris, T. W. and Peeters, M. C. (2007) Take Care! The evaluation of a team-based burnout intervention program for oncology care providers. *Journal of Applied Psychology* 92: 213–27.

Lederberg, M. S. (1998) Staff support groups for high-stress medical environments. *International Journal of Group Psychotherapy* 48: 275–304.

Main, T. F. (1957) The ailment. *British Journal of Medical Psychology* 30: 129–35.

Main, T. (1990) Knowledge, learning and freedom from thought. *Psychoanalytic Psychotherapy* 5: 59–78.

Malan, D. (1979) *Individual Psychotherapy and the Science of Psychodynamics*. London: Butterworth.

Marrone, M. (1998) *Attachment and Interaction*. London: Jessica Kingsley.

Menzies, I. E. P. (1959) The functioning of social systems as a defence against anxiety. *Human Relations* 13: 95–121.

Milton, J. and Davison, S. (1997) Observations of staff support groups with time limited external facilitation in a psychiatric institution. *Psychoanalytic Psychotherapy* 11: 135–45.

Molnos, A. (1995) *A Question of Time*. London: Karnac.

Moos, R. H. (1986) *Work Environmental Scale Manual*, 2nd edn. Palo Alto, CA: Consulting Psychologists Press.

Moos, R. H. (1997) *Evaluating Treatment Environments: The Quality of Psychiatric and Substance Abuse Programmes*. New Brunswick: Transaction Publishers.

Moylan, D. (2006) The dangers of contagion: Projective identification processes in institutes. In A. Obholzer and V. Z. Roberts (eds) *The Unconscious at Work: Individual and Organisational Stress in the Human Services*. London: Routledge.

Music, G. (2007) Learning our lessons: some issues arising from delivering mental health services in schools. *Psychoanalytic Psychotherapy* 21: 1–19.

National Institute for Mental Health in England (2003) *Personality Disorder: No Longer a Diagnosis for Exclusion*. London: Department of Health.

Nitsun, M. (1996) *The Anti Group: Destructive Forces in the Group and their Creative Potential.* London: Routledge.

Obholzer, A. and Roberts, V. Z. (2006) *The Unconscious at Work: Individual and Organisational Stress in the Human Services.* London: Routledge.

Olofsson, B. (2005) Opening up: psychiatric nurses experiences of participating in reflection groups focussing on the use of coercion. *Journal of Psychiatric and Mental Health Nursing* 12: 259–67.

Oxford English Dictionary (1992) Oxford: Oxford University Press.

Pines, M. (1983) *The Evolution of Group Analysis.* London: Routledge.

Pines, M. (1991) Interminable patients. In J. Roberts and M. Pines *The Practice of Group Analysis.* London: Routledge.

Proctor, B. (2000) *Group Supervision: A Guide to Creative Practice.* London: Sage.

Punter, J. (2007) A commentary on Ashton. *Group Analysis* 40: 96–101.

Schon, D. (1984) *The Reflective Practitioner: How Professionals Think in Action.* New York: Basic Books.

Rance, C. (1989) What has group analysis to offer in the context of organisational consultancy? *Group Analysis* 22: 333–43.

Reid, Y., Johnson, S., Morant, N., Kuipers, E., Szmukler, G., Bebbington, P., Thornicroft, G. and Prosser, D. (1999) Improving support for mental health staff: a qualitative study. *Social Psychiatry and Psychiatric Epidemiology* 34: 309–15.

Rifkind, G. (1995) Containing the container: The staff consultation group. *Group Analysis* 28: 209–22.

Ritter, S., Tolchard, B. and Stewart, R. (1995) Coping with stress in mental health nursing. In J. Carsin, L. Fagin and S. Ritter (eds) *Stress and Coping in Mental Health Nursing.* London: Chapman and Hall.

Robertson, S. and Davison, S. (1997) A survey of groups within a psychiatric hospital. *Psychoanalytic Psychotherapy* 11: 119–33.

Ryan, A. and Pritchard, J. (2004) *Good Practice in Adult Mental Health.* London: Jessica Kingsley.

Sourander, A., Aromaa, M., Pihlakoski, L., Haavisto, A., Rautava, P., Helenius, H. and Sillanpää, M. (2006) Early predictors of deliberate self-harm among adolescents. A prospective follow-up study from age 3 to age 15. *Journal of Affective Disorders* 93: 87–96.

Thomas, P. (1995) A study of the effectiveness of staff support groups. *Nursing Times* 91: 36–9.

Thomas, P. (2001) Professional development through supervision and staff groups. In P. Thomas, S. Davison and C. Rance (eds) *Clinical Counselling in Medical Settings.* London: Routledge.

Thomas, P. (2003) A study of the effectiveness of professional development groups. *Nursing Times* 99: 32–4.

Tillett, R. (2003) The patient within – psychopathology in the helping professions. *Advances in Psychiatric Treatment* 9: 272–9.

Tommasini, N. R. (1992) The impact of a staff support group on the work environment of a specialty unit. *Archives of Psychiatric Nursing* 6: 40–7.

Whitaker, D. S. (1992) Transposing learnings from group psychotherapy to work groups. *Group Analysis* 25: 131–49.

Winnicott, D. W. (1971) *Playing and Reality.* London: Tavistock.

Winnicott, D. W. (1992) Hate in the countertransference. In D. W. Winnicott *Through Paediatrics to Psychoanalysis*. New York: Brunner-Routledge.

Winship, G. (1995) The unconscious impact of caring for acutely disturbed patients. *Journal of Psychiatric and Mental Health Nursing* 2: 227–33.

Winship, G. (2005) Consciousness raising in public sphere organisations. *Psychoanalytic Psychotherapy* 19: 233–45.

Winship, G. (2007) *Taking Anarchy Seriously*. Paper presented at ATC (Association of Therapeutic Communities) Annual Windsor Conferences: Institutions for Chaos. Sept 4th 2007. (www.winship.info/anarchy).

Winship, G. and Hardy, S. (1999) Disentangling group dynamics: staff group sensitivity and supervision. *Journal of Psychiatric and Mental Health Nursing* 6: 307–12.

Yalom, I. (1985) *The Theory and Practice of Group Psychotherapy*, 4th edn. New York: Basic Books.

Author index

Subject index